Intercultural Communication

Under the advisory editorship of J. Jeffery Auer

Intercultural Communication

L. S. Harms
University of Hawaii

Harper & Row, Publishers
New York, Evanston, San Francisco, London

Sponsoring Editor: Voras D. Meeks
Project Editor: Ralph Cato
Designer: Michel Craig
Production Supervisor: Stefania J. Taflinska

Standard Book Number: 06-042644-6

Library of Congress Catalog Card Number: 73-8499

The Japanese *haiku* appearing on page ix is reprinted by permission of Charles E. Tuttle Co., Inc., from *A Net of Fireflies* by Harold Stewart.

for Joan Yukino

Contents

Preface

CHAIN MAIL
A chestnut dropped in.
A goldfish rose to drink.
Their widening rings of water interlink.
Kijiro

Men of vision, like U Thant and John F. Kennedy, have understood that we humans must seek a common long-range goal: to ensure *cultural diversity* and *human variety* upon our small planet. *Intercultural Communication* attempts to advance this goal.

The book was drafted during a sabbatical study tour and developed during more than a decade of research, teaching, and practical experience in the area of intercultural communication. The first few chapters and several of the later units were written in Geneva. Other units and subunits were drafted in London, Paris, Istanbul, Delhi, Hong Kong, Tokyo, Honolulu, and elsewhere in the world. The actual writing was done in hotel rooms, cafés, parks, public libraries, and airplanes.

The text is written for the beginning student of intercultural communication. It is organized into five major sections. Chapters 1–3 provide a general foundation for the study. They are intended to be read first and in sequence. Chapters 4–7 are devoted to the specific topics of intercommunity communication, international communication, world communication, and future trends of intercultural communication. These may be read in any desired order. Appendix 1 sets forth the ideals of the United Nations regarding human dignity and cultural diversity. These lofty principles, when considered from both philosophical and realistic standpoints, may provide the source for stimulating class discussions. A number of student projects are outlined in Appendix 2. They enable the reader to explore in detail those concepts he finds of greatest interest. When the student has completed these projects, he will have mastered an integral part of the content of the book. A thorough bibliography of important and contemporary books and articles concludes the text.

A few of the problems of intercultural communication are identified and examined. Yet the emphasis of this text is not the *problems* so much as the *possibilities* that await the communicator who engages successfully in intercultural communication. This book is written for the cautious optimist. *Aloha.*

L. S. Harms

Acknowledgments

This book has evolved through the type of communication called intercultural interchange. Thus, my debt to other people is unusually large. In particular, the central concepts developed in this book began to take shape in the course of a series of long discussions with Inayatullah at the East–West Center in Honolulu. Others who were particularly helpful at one time or another include Carl Landé, Peter Iizuka, Manfred Schröder, Yukio Takefuta, Fred Casmir, Kwan Tan, Paul Heinberg, Hans J. Tillman, Alejandro Casambre, Michikazu Kaneda, Gerald Dykstra, Frank Johnson, William S. Howell, and Florangel Rosario.

Both Dr. Howell and Dr. Rosario were kind enough to read the manuscript and offer helpful suggestions. In addition, several of the students enrolled in my Intercultural Seminar read the manuscript and commented on it; I would particularly like to thank Kathleen Busick, Art Challacombe, Mu-Lan Hsu, Margo MacLeod, Monina Movido, Queenie Mow, Benjamin Tayabas, and John White. I am grateful to the Ford Foundation for the opportunity to begin this book through an International Curriculum Grant to the University of Kansas administered by Dr. Francis Heller. I am also indebted to the University of Hawaii for the sabbatical leave that made it possible to complete the book.

I would like also to thank Lu Russell, my Waikiki Secretary, for a commendable job of manuscript typing. To Voras D. Meeks, and a "few of his friends" at Harper & Row, I would like again to say: Thank you! Finally, to Miss Kathleen Ayumi Kie, *ichiban* student assistant: *mahalo* and *aloha*.

Intercultural Communication

1

Worldview of Human Communication

Our task in this first chapter is to develop a perspective that is broad enough to encompass the *full range* of problems and possibilities which form the core of intercultural communication. Let us call that perspective a *worldview.* Such a worldview extends through time, stretches across space, and provides a framework for sketching the *story* of intercultural communication. As this story unfolds, we must account for the fact that an increasing proportion of human communication is intercultural communication, and some of that intercultural communication achieves vital purposes.

Intercultural communication arises from two simple and related facts. Man can talk across distances of a few yards. Man can walk across distances of a few miles. And he can, of course, talk and walk at the same time. Talking and walking seem to us modest accomplishments, at a time when we have grown accustomed to having men walk on the moon and talk with us as they are doing so. But when taken together, talking and walking do provide a useful and simple starting point for our study of intercultural communication. Let us begin at the beginning of human communication.

INTRODUCTION

Half a million years ago, through gradual stages, man developed the skills necessary to communicate with his fellowman. It is not yet known how man first learned to communicate. It is clear, however, that communication skills have been maintained and relearned for thousands upon thousands of years, in each of the small communities of the world. No community is without its networks and systems of communication. Almost all of the human experience in communication remains anchored in the small home community of a few hundred or a few thousand people.

The relationship between communication and culture is a rich and delicate one. It is rich in the sense that communication and culture are intertwined at almost every point. It is delicate in the sense that a change in either communication or culture is likely to produce a related change in the other. In this book I make a distinction between communication and culture, although other authors writing in this area (Hall, Edward T., 1959:93; Smith, A., 1966) have preferred to treat them as inseparable. As we progress through the book the distinction will become increasingly important, especially in the last chapter dealing with future developments, where both communication and culture are stretched beyond their customary meanings.

Questions of similarities and of differences will arise frequently in the following pages. Communication among members of a community—*intra*cultural communication—promotes those similarities identified as part of a shared culture. Communication between members of two (or several) different communities—*inter*cultural communication—reveals the differences or nonshared details of culture. Thus, the judgment of *same* or *different* has a central place in the study of intercultural communication.

Some of the most important similarities and differences are explored in a number of case studies. They range from the social dialect transformation undertaken by Eliza Doolittle and Henry Higgins to the challenge that awaits us when we first engage in communication with intelligent life from outer space. I hope that one or more of these cases provides you with a starting point for a more detailed study of intercultural communication. The projects at the end of the book will help you display some of the many important details and patterns that can only be hinted at in this book.

As an area of study, intercultural communication is quite new. Those of us who consider this area to be one of our major interests are not in agreement on many essential points. There are, for instance, a thousand or more definitions of culture (Girard, 1972) and a hundred or more definitions of communication (Dance, 1970:201). Several books—collections of articles—published recently contain very few of the same articles, even though all of these books focus on intercultural communication. In the Bibliography, for instance, see the books by Prosser (1973), Smith (1972), Samover and Porter (1972), and Triandis (1972).

The differences in approach, definition, and viewpoint are obvious. Those differences do not worry me, and they should not worry you. For those differences are but one more instance of cultural diversity, and cultural diversity, as we shall see, remains a very good and necessary thing.

Time/Space Review

Let us discover again where we are. Our planet has a life expectancy of about nine billion years. Our good earth is about four and one-half billion years old. In a form that can be called human, man has walked about the surface of the earth for only a few million years. Man has been able to talk for a brief half-million years. Talking man is a newcomer on a middle-aged planet. Figure 1 illustrates that human communication history is still a very short story compared to the history of the earth.

At about the time that man learned to talk, his brain increased in size. It is a peculiar fact that man has learned to use only a small percentage of his brain capacity. By contrast, the appendix once served a storage function; but now, with three meals a day routinely available, the appendix can be safely removed. An arm or a leg can be replaced by artificial limbs. A kidney can be removed from one person and implanted in another. But the gray matter that makes up the human brain is indispensable. Much of the brain remains unused as yet—awaiting something. Further

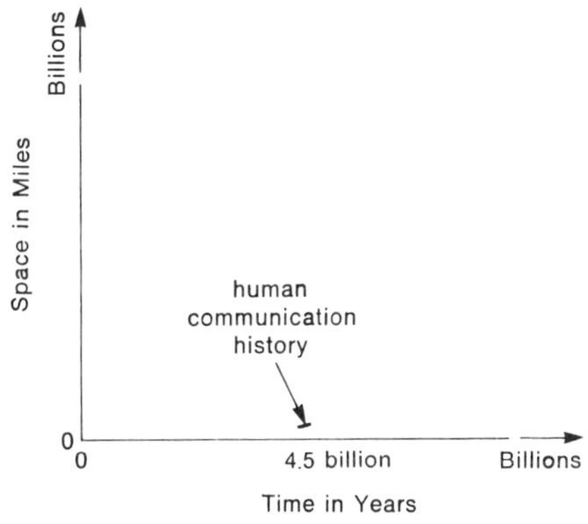

Figure 1 Human communication history

development of human brain capacity, perhaps, can come through intercultural communication (Lenneberg, 1967:70; Ruzic, 1970).

Intercultural communication makes it possible for any man to learn what any other man knows, what several other men know, and perhaps, what all men have known, now know, or will know. More importantly, any two or several men with differing cultural backgrounds have the possibility—the unique opportunity—of inventing and creating new information. Taken together, these possibilities of discovering what many others know and inventing new information may yet utilize the excess capacity of that underdeveloped area between the left ear and the right ear! In the future, as a minimum, it may be possible for any man to be as wise as all men, and as a maximum to be very much more.

When I consider the possibilities, I am a bit overwhelmed. Perhaps you are, too. But we humans are very young. Our past is relatively short; our future can be *billions* of years long! The advances we make will depend on the success we have in this new adventure of intercultural communication.

Change

Our world is changing at a shocking rate. In recent years, we have invented two new terms to describe that change: culture-shock and future-shock. Culture-shock describes the condition, the disease, experienced by a person suddenly transplanted into a foreign culture (Arensberg and Niehoff, 1971:233). Future-shock describes the experience of the person who finds "things" in his own community changing so fast he is no longer able to deal with them (Toffler, 1971). In their extreme forms, both types of shock can result in physical or mental illness.

But not all of the communities of the world change at the same rate; there is diversity in rate of change, too. Take the matter of human population as an illustration. In 1800, the world's population numbered 1 billion. By 1970, that number had grown to 3.6 billion. At the present world growth rate of 2.1 percent, the world population will number 6 billion by the year 2000 (Meadows and others, 1972). Any particular small community, where we humans live out our lives, may have a pattern at substantial variance with the world cultural patterns. Many rural communities cease to exist as community members migrate to a nearby city; or, in a reversal of that process, new towns may be developed. The variations are endless, and for intercultural communication, this is the important point.

Human communication is greatly influenced by world trends in the educational, economic, and social areas, but it is also influenced by the quality of life reflected in the many small communities of the world. Most humans learn to communicate in their own home community, within the framework provided by their local culture. Further, there is a variety of communication styles among the members of a given community. Diversity exists. Variety exists. And that diversity in culture and variety in communication is what makes intercultural communication both difficult and important.

WORLD COMMUNICATION REVOLUTIONS

In the short history of man, there have been at least five major communication revolutions. Each of these revolutions created many new possibilities and introduced a few new problems as well. Any major change in communication tends to have far-reaching effects on a world scale.

Speech

The ability to communicate through speech is held to be one of the distinguishing characteristics of man. There is no agreement as to when or how man first developed skill in speech communication. At present, the best time estimate seems to be approximately 500,000 years ago. How man learned to talk is even less certain. There are many theories or semitheories about this matter that have delightful names, such as *Bow Wow* and *Ding Dong* (Gray and Wise, 1959:455). All that is known is that every human community has a well-developed system for speech communication, and that these systems of communication differ enough from community to community to be called by different names, such as English, Swahili, French, Urdu, Tagalog, Japanese, Mandarin, German, Maori, Arabic, Slovak, Norwegian . . . and several thousand more.

The capacity for speech communication in any community opens up several possibilities. First of all, it enables community members to coordinate activities as diverse as hunting food, managing a household, and planning to sow grain. Division of labor becomes possible. A new level of human association or interpersonal relationship also becomes possible. In addition, men can talk over things that have happened and come to understand them better. Men can also use speech to plan the future.

With the development of speech, timelessness ended. Man could coordinate activities in the present, reinterpret the past, and plan the future. Today, when more than 90 percent of the children in the world are skilled communicators within their home community by age five, it is easy to underestimate the significance of speech communication. Yet its absence, as in deafness or mental disorders, underscores the necessary role it plays in daily life.

A further point should be made. By 1800, the world population had just reached 1 billion. Almost all of those persons lived in small communities. In 1800, the largest city in the world was London, and its population was less than a million. New York City's population was a very large 60,000. About 90 percent of the U.S. population lived in small communities and was engaged mainly in agriculture. Only 170 years later, the New York City population numbered almost 8 million, and fewer than 10 percent of the U.S. population was engaged in agriculture. In human terms, the growth in population size and the movement from country to city has been very rapid. By contrast, human patterns of communication have evolved very slowly in a comparatively small community. Almost all of our communication inheritance is *pretechnological* (Hall, Peter, 1966).

Writing

After speech developed about one-half million years ago, there was a long period when little new in communication seems to have happened. Perhaps it took one-half million years to fully develop and refine speech. And, quite likely there were other developments we have no hint of today.

About 3000 B.C., in Sumer or Mesopotamia, a well-developed writing system is known to have existed. In the Room of Writing in the British Museum in London, the emergence of writing is charted on the four walls of the room. The first clay tablets with marks made by a reed pen—the first instrument, the beginning of technology—are displayed. An alternate form of writing on stone with a chisel is shown. Finally, paper and pen make a portable book possible.

Writing introduces the possibility of storing information with greater precision than is possible by the human memory, for a period of time longer than a man's life. Writing also creates the necessity of learning to read. While the communication skills of speaking and listening are normally learned at home before age five, reading and writing remain, for the most part, school subjects. Formal training seems to be required. Yet the accomplishments of reading and writing, when contrasted with speaking and listening, seem modest indeed. Perhaps it is only that in human history, writing and reading are relatively new skills.

In the communities of the world, a very large number of persons can neither write nor read. One UNESCO estimate places the number of persons unable to write or read at nearly 1 billion, or approximately half of the adult population of the world (McHale, 1972:83).

Printing

The invention of the printing press occurred in Germany, between 1440 and 1455. The first printed book was the Christian Bible, and it was placed on sale in 1455. The man most responsible for the galaxy of printed material that engulfs us today is Johann Gutenberg of Mainz. The story of the invention of the first printing press equals, in intrigue, any story ever printed.

The printing press was first recognized as a better way of reproducing manuscripts than the slow and inaccurate method of copying by hand. While the printing press and the more recent photocopying machines continue to be used for the reproduction of manuscripts, a number of effects of Gutenberg's invention are apparent. The printing press makes it possible for any desired number of copies of a message to be *set* in print. Truth, as well as error, becomes fixed as if cut into stone.

The printing press introduced a number of controls into human communication. The controls were all possible on a small scale after the development of writing, but it was in the extension made possible by the printing press that the controls became evident. In particular, all books, magazines, and newspapers are written by relatively few people. The information set down by these writers tends to be that which is known by the members of a particular community and becomes part of the literature of many communities.

Thus, a first control is introduced because most of what is printed is written by a small number of people. An additional control exists in that currently half of the adults in the world cannot yet read.

Print does make it possible, however, to preserve and widely distribute matters of general interest, such as constitutions, religious works, great literature from ancient times, and so on. All of these and many other printed items shape human cultures.

Mobility

In the hundred-year span between 1870 and 1970, the capacity of man to walk and talk over distances has been extended to the point that earth distance ceases to be a major constraint on human communication.

The century just past has been unique and unprecedented in the communication history of man. Hundreds of inventions and developments, each remarkable enough in its own right to start a revolution in some other age, followed one another in rapid succession. In the transportation area, steamships, transcontinental railroads, automobiles, and airplanes came into use as an extension of walking. In the telecommunication area, the newspaper press, telephone, telegraph, radio and television broadcasting, and the satellite came into use as an extension of talking (*From Semaphore to Satellite*, 1965). What is more, various of the transportation and telecommunication technologies are used in combination by the communicator on the move. Police cars in every city are examples, as are the jets that arrive at and depart from every major airport. Teleportation may be close at hand!

There is, as yet, no single term for the revolution of transportation and telecommunication technologies. The term *mobile* was selected because it points to the removal or reduction of time and space constraints on the communication activities of man. Significantly, the reduction of these constraints sets the stage for the revolution in human communication that is just beginning—the intercultural communication revolution (Cherry, 1971).

Intercultural Communication

The intercultural communication revolution is a *participant* or grass-roots revolution. It is characterized by two-way communication between persons from diverse communities. It relies more on the telephone than radio and television, more on dialogue than public speech. This revolution is characterized by cooperative, rather than competitive, modes of communication. It is just now getting underway.

As the intercultural communication revolution gains momentum, a number of its characteristics become apparent. First of all, there are two significant levels of culture: a world macroculture and community-based local microcultures. This division has been evident to some observers for a long while, but it was obscured for a time by certain goals of the nation state. The American "melting pot," for instance, was intended to forge a new man made in America (Glazer and Moynihan, 1970:288). On the surface, and for a time, this appeared to be happening. But an interest in the global and the universal world culture grows at the same time that there is a community-by-community revival of the little, local culture (Barth, 1969).

A reexamination of communication patterns reveals a similar set of trends. At the same time that there is a rapid and marked growth in world communication, there is an intensification of communication within the local community. Thus, the jet plane and the compact car, the communication satellite and the wired community, the world man and the ethnic man developed at the same time. Rather than evolving to a global village, we evolve the global community and the village and interlink those two cultures by intercultural communication (Cherry, 1971).

WORLD COMMUNICATION NETWORKS

We began with the simple observation that man can walk about the surface of the earth and talk to other men across short distances. Within a community of a few hundred or even a few thousand people, any man can talk to any other man. To be sure, even in a small, stable community, custom will require that some men not talk to others, that some men speak only when spoken to, and so on. Within a small community, then, communication among the community members can be adequately served by the twin abilities of being able to walk across and talk across short distances.

Communication between members of two neighboring communities would be possible under certain conditions, but it can quickly become a problem of such magnitude that it is undertaken seldom, if at all. For instance, a man on foot can walk 10 miles to a neighboring community, spend a few hours exchanging information, and return home by nightfall. A journey to a community 100 miles distant, even on horseback is one to be reckoned in days, and it would take longer to reach a community 1,000 miles distant on horseback than it now takes a spaceship to travel from the earth to the moon. For most of man's history, his boots have been used for walking relatively short distances.

Similar observations can be made of man's capacity to communicate across distances. Normal conversation is carried on across distances of a few feet. Loud talk carries 50 feet on a quiet day. Shouting can cover a distance of 100 feet or more—but not much more. Smoke signals, when the wind is down and the sun is up, and drum talk, when the wind is down and the terrain is flat, extend the distance across which man can communicate with his fellowman in a nearby community. But the smoke signal and the drum are not very reliable (*From Semaphore to Satellite*, 1965).

By contrast, what has happened in just the last few years is that it has become possible for any man to travel in the period from one sunrise to the next sunrise to any other community in the world. Equally, it has become possible, within a few minutes, for any one man to communicate via telephone with any other man in any other community. To be sure, there are exceptions. But they are *exceptions*—and temporary ones. In both cases, two-way communication is possible, it is possible on a very large scale, and large-scale, two-way communication between persons in diverse communities is a new thing in the world. Large-scale, two-way communication between members of diverse communities is the central force in the revolution of intercultural communication.

There are now two world-communication networks. The first of these is a telecommunication network; it extends the capacity of man to talk across distances. The second is a transportation network; it extends the capacity of man to move across distance. Together, these two networks provide the global framework necessary to understand the problems and possibilities of intercultural communication.

Telecomnet

Telecomnet is the abbreviation for the Telecommunication Network. For the study of intercultural communication, the telephone and the communication satellite are the important related items of technology. It will be important, from time to time, to refer to radio and television, but these "mass media" are one-way devices and are of secondary importance to intercultural communication. Our central concern is with two-way communication between members of different communities.

Once a particular item of communication technology comes into use in a community, it is easy to forget both how things were before and that members of other communities may not yet have access to it. The telephone provides a useful example. In the United States, in 1971, more than 30 billion telephone calls were made. A very high percentage of these calls were essentially *within community* calls. They were conversations carried on over a *short distance*. For the most part, they were calls between persons who knew each other and who communicated about local matters of family, business, and the like. As it is presently used, the telephone serves to reinforce values, beliefs, and action patterns of a community—in a word, its culture.

There is, however, a counter trend. Before the mid-1950s, transoceanic telephone calls depended on a two-way radio link. If atmospheric conditions were favorable, such communication was satisfactory. Often, of course, the conversation would fade in and out, making normal communication difficult or impossible. In 1956, the first transatlantic telephone cable was laid. It had the capacity to carry several two-way telephone conversations at a time. Within twelve months, that cable was being used to capacity, and an additional cable was laid with a much larger capacity for voice channels. In twelve months it, too, was being fully used. Much the same story holds for the Pacific. The first transpacific cable stretched from San Francisco through Honolulu and Guam and on to Tokyo. Only a few months after it was put into operation, its channels were being fully used. Lest the point be lost, nearly all transoceanic telephone calls are fundamental examples of intercultural communication.

The experience with transoceanic telephone cable has been that as new channels become available, they are soon used at or near capacity. People from widely separated communities talk to each other when they are able to do so. But laying cables across ocean floors is expensive to the degree that they must be laid only between large and populous communities—in practice, between the large cities of the world.

At present, a distinction is made between local (or short-distance) calls and long-distance calls. That distinction is made, in part, because each foot of cable costs an additional amount to install and maintain. But we must now consider a quite different situation, one in which all calls are either local or long-distance, depending on how you choose to view the matter. In other words, cost ceases to be influenced by earth distance between communicators.

The communication satellite is now about a decade old. The first Early Bird was placed in orbit over the Atlantic in 1965. It had only a few two-way voice channels and a useful life of a few years. Early Bird was followed by larger satellites with many more two-way voice channels. The Intelsat IV satellite has many channels and an expected life span of a dozen years. What is more, any desired number of new satellites of even greater capacity can be built in a few months and placed in orbit in a few minutes, to be available for almost instant use. Within the Soviet Union, Japan, France, England, the United States, and other countries, the capabilities exist to build as many satellites as are needed.

One part of the communication satellite story has to do with the rapid increase in channels for telephone and other uses. An equally important part has to do with the relationship between cost and distance. A satellite is placed in orbit 22,300 miles above the equator. Three satellites strategically positioned, that is, one over the Atlantic, another over the Pacific, and a third over the Indian Ocean, provide virtually total coverage of the land and water surface of the earth. Using one or, at most, two of these three satellites, it is possible to connect any two telephones in the world. To be sure, some additional ground equipment is needed. The essential point is that the distance the "call" travels ceases to be important. Every call can span 44,600 miles *or a little more.* Telephone calls by satellite are essentially "distance free."

The present long-distance rates do not yet reflect the savings brought about by the satellite. There are a number of ways that you could change that. In the meantime, we have a little while to consider the probable consequences of large-scale, two-way, worldwide telephone communication on the communities of man. Add also the fact that quite soon telephone will be accompanied by a video component, a shift comparable to that from radio to television. Well before the year 2000, perhaps by 1980, worldwide videophone will be available for a modest monthly rental (Martin, 1971).

Transcomnet

Transcomnet is the abbreviation used for the term *transportation communication network.* For our study of intercultural communication, the automobile and the jet plane are the important related items of technology. At times, we will need to consider trains, buses, boats, space shuttles, and other means of transporting humans, but these vehicles are of secondary importance in the study of intercultural communication at this time. Our central concern remains two-way communication between members of different and distant communities.

Automobiles came into use after major factories for their production were built in the 1920s and 1930s. About a half-century later there are traffic jams in the United States and elsewhere in the world. The United States is linked by thousands of miles of interstate highways and by countless miles of city streets, rural roads, and other auto pathways. For the most part, for distances of more than a few city blocks, the auto replaces walking as a means of transportation. Most of the miles driven per year are accumulated during short trips of just a few miles within the home community.

The present pattern of automobile use parallels that of the local telephone call. The short auto trip and the local telephone call both serve to strengthen and maintain cultural patterns within a community.

Some of the major roadways in every community lead to the local airport. For a trip of more than a few hundred miles, especially as highways become more congested, the alternative of flying instead of driving becomes attractive. A major amount of time in any travel by plane is utilized in driving to the airport, getting on the plane, getting off the plane, and driving on to the final destination. For most long flights from most major cities, nearly two hours elapse from the time the traveler leaves home until the plane lifts off the ground. Most of the costs involved are costs necessitated on or near the ground, that is, in ground passenger services, takeoff and landing fuel costs, aircraft ground time, and so on. As in the cost of the long-distance phone call, the cost of air *distance* becomes of decreasing importance.

Long-distance, transoceanic flights have been available on a regularly scheduled hour for only a few years. Charles A. Lindbergh flew the Atlantic for the first time in the twenties. The first China

Clippers flew from San Francisco to Honolulu, and regular service was established. Today, on the West Coast–Hawaii route, eight major airlines each fly one, and some several, large—707 or 747—planes per day. The growth in long-distance air traffic resembles the growth in long-distance telephone traffic.

On the longer transoceanic flights, the increase in air traffic has doubled on the average of every few years. Over both the Atlantic and the Pacific, the growth in passenger traffic has exceeded most predictions by a wide margin. It is not yet clear where air travel will level off. If it were to continue to double every few years, in a very short time all several billion of us would be flying all the time, which, at the moment, seems to be going a bit too far.

The satellite promises to change the cost of using the telephone to talk over long distances. A similar move to make cost only partly dependent on distance is underway in air travel. The charter flights, which fly only with a full plane, are able to offer seats on long flights for about half the regular fare. These reduced rates are making it possible for persons who, in an earlier time, would not have been able to afford it, to travel outside their communities and countries.

Within the field of air travel, there are several developments underway which are likely to further reduce cost per distance. One of these, of course, is the bigger, faster, supersonic transport. Beyond that are suborbital craft which make any two airports on earth essentially of the same space/time distance. That is, it will take about twenty minutes to travel from any one airport to any other airport. Under such a plan, obviously, there would be either a single fare or no fare at all.

Air travel, then, makes it possible for any human to travel to a distant community within a very few hours. Conversely, strangers from distant communities will, with increasing frequency, arrive at the community airport, stay for a time in hotels, and exchange information within the community. In both cases, a much higher percentage of the ten hours per day most people spend communicating will be spent in intercultural communication. *We do not yet know the long-term consequences of too little, the right amount of, or too much intercultural communication.*

All of this traveling over long distances in short times is a very recent thing. The human body does not respond quickly to changes in time zone and climate, as every traveler who suffers jet fatigue knows painfully. In an earlier time, Odysseus the Greek could write his *Odyssey.* The fictional Gulliver could report in sober tones what happened in Lilliput and Laputa. Marco Polo could journey to China and return with the riches of the Orient. Today, the college student may, in the course of a summer trip, see the seven wonders of the world and return in the fall with slides to show and tales to tell. But he does not rent a hall and charge admission; he is lucky to have a few friends and family members with the interest to see and hear.

There are now two great communication networks that encircle the globe. The first of these is the telecomnet, built from the telephone and related switching equipment and the communication satellite. The second network is the transcomnet, built from the automobile and airport and the jet plane. The telecomnet permits communicators to interchange information over any desired distance while remaining in their home communities. The transcomnet enables any communicator to travel to any other community and, on a face-to-face basis, interchange information. Taken together, these two world networks extend the possibility for two-way communication far beyond what was expected even ten years ago. In a cryptic way, Colin Cherry poses the essential question, World communication: threat or promise? (Cherry, 1971).

COMMUNICATION SYSTEMS

The two world communication networks—the telecomnet and the transcomnet—exist whether they are under heavy use, moderate use, or no use at all at a particular moment. The satellite does not fall from the sky if none of its channels are being used to carry telephone conversations. Jet planes fly their scheduled routes with passengers in every seat or with so few passengers a stewardess or two must join the passengers to make a foursome for bridge. To be sure, the capacity of each network to serve the demands of human communication can be increased and decreased from time to time. But the basic network structure continues to be available for use, and that is the critical matter.

Another major distinction is now required. The two communication *networks* are built out of the telecommunication and transportation technologies. These networks depend on *hardware.* The three communication *systems* are organized by humans to achieve a mutual purpose. These systems are built from human software.

The three basic human communication systems are the dyad, organized by two communicators; the small group, organized by seven plus or minus two communicators; and the large group, organized by seven times two plus *n* communicators, or more simply, by fifteen or more communicators. By definition, each of these systems operates within one of the two networks to achieve some purpose.

The Dyad

The dyad is organized by two and only two human communicators to achieve some mutual purpose. It is also known as person-to-person communication, a conversational pair, a two-group, a speaker–listener pair, one-to-one communication, a two-person system, and by several other names (Jaffe and Feldstein, 1970).

When the dyad operates in a telecomnet, that communication is usually referred to as a telephone call or a phone conversation. In our terms, it is a dyadic communication system operating in a telecomnet. The distinction between network and system becomes very useful a little later on.

When the dyad operates in a transcomnet, that communication is usually called a conversation or dialog. In our terms, it is a dyadic system operating in a transcomnet. If all communication were limited by the walk–talk capabilities of man, as described earlier, there would be little point in distinguishing between systems and network. But now that the communication networks remove a number of time and distance constraints, it becomes useful to spell

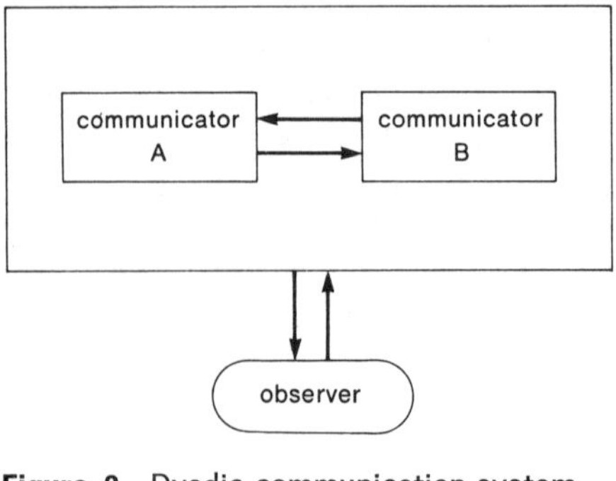

Figure 2 Dyadic communication system

out these changes clearly enough to identify and analyze the consequences for intercultural communication.

One such consequence of the network/system distinction can be observed in daily patterns of communication within a community. Given an average communication day of ten hours per community member, any community member may elect to spend all his time communicating with persons who are nearby and well known, that is, organize dyads employing transcomnet links of 100 feet or less. Another community member may devote 30 percent of his communication time to telecomnet links of 1,000 miles or more, 50 percent of his time to telecomnet links of about 50 miles beyond the community, and 20 percent of his time in very short transcomnet links in his home community. The rate of cultural change of the first person would be very slow; that of the second person relatively rapid. The length of these network links is associated with rate of change.

In Chapter 3 we will consider the intercultural dyad in some detail. It is the most important system for intercultural communication.

The Small Group

The small group is organized by seven (± 2) communicators to achieve some mutual purpose. It is also called a discussion group, a team, a committee, a conference call, and other names.

When the small group operates in a telecomnet, that communication is usually labeled a conference call or group conference. In our terms, it is a small group communication system operating in a telecomnet.

When the small group operates in a transcomnet, that communication is usually called a discussion. In our terms, it is a small group communication system operating in a transcomnet.

For intercultural communication, the small group ranks behind the dyad in importance. However, within the 2,500 assorted major world organizations, the small group in both networks becomes increasingly important.

The Large Group

The large group usually includes fifteen or more communicators. Usually only one or a few of these communicators are involved in the major decisions of organization. The large group is almost entirely a one-way system. It is also called a public speech, a lecture, a radio broadcast, a television program, a reading, and other names.

When the large group operates in a telecomnet, that communication is usually called a radio or television broadcast. In our terms, these mass media broadcasts are a large group communication system operating in a telecomnet.

When the large group operates in a transcomnet, that communication is usually called a public speech or a lecture. In our terms, it is a large group communication system operating in a transcomnet.

For intercultural communication, the large group ranks far behind the dyad and the small group in importance. At this point in history, it is not yet easy to state precisely why this is so. But let us try.

First, the large group systems are one-way systems. A message is prepared, and that prepared message is transmitted to a group of receiver–communicators. Usually, the more the better. In the realm of intercultural communication, large group communication focuses on transmitting messages from a central source to the members of several communities. Quite often, the central source is a government or government agency attempting to gain support for and adoption of its policies and programs. A certain amount of such communication is clearly necessary to maintain the nation state. But the satellite and jet *may* have already made nations obsolete.

More to the point, there is always a time trade-off in communication. Time spent as a receiver–communicator of radio and TV broadcasts is time not spent in other types of communication. In general, even from information programs, such as a newscast, most of what any person receives is not news to him. He wastes time listening, in much the same way that persons in the traditional village waste time in idle chatter and gossip. When there are no alternatives to the mass media, perhaps these systems are beneficial.

But it is a hard fact of life that all large group systems do not operate to the equal and mutual benefit of all communicators participating in the system. The soap opera and the violent Western broadcast to sell soap and deodorant are natural consequences. So are the political uses to sow hate and distrust and fear throughout a nation. Fortunately, the satellite and the jet make several better alternatives possible. We shall explore some of these better possibilities in the remainder of the book.

NETWORKS	transcomnet	telecomnet
SYSTEMS	dyad small group large group	dyad small group large group

Figure 3 Systems in networks

Systems in Networks

Each of the three systems can operate in either of the two networks. In the dyad and the small group, most often, the communicators themselves decide in what size system they will communicate, in which of the two networks they will communicate, and in general, they are free to decide and act. In sharp contrast, the large group system is usually organized by only a small percentage of the communicators involved. In most cases, the organizers stand to benefit more than any of the other participants. Those participants who serve as receiver–communicators have very little say in the total operation of the system. They can participate or not, switch from one channel to another, change radio stations, not attend a lecture, or walk out on a public speaker. However, these techniques do not in any systematic way serve to improve communication. See Figure 3.

For the purposes of intercultural communication, the give-and-take of two-way communication is of central importance. It makes possible the exchange or interchange of information and attitudes.

PURPOSE IN A SYSTEM/NETWORK

Sometimes it appears that everyone is communicating with everyone else all the time. Waltzlawick and others (1967) argue that man in the presence of another man cannot *not communicate.* From one point of view, that is true. But to consider everything a human does as communication makes communication an unwieldy thing.

The concept of purpose, or intent, or goal seeking is among the most difficult in the study of human communication, and it is important especially in the area of intercultural communication. Robert Oliver captures the essence of the problem:

In the West the purpose has been considered the factor in the speaking situation which above all was to be dominated by the speaker . . . seeking to influence listeners in the direction of his own convictions. To abridge or amend his purpose in order to win audience approval was considered a serious breach of ethics. . . . Again and again [for the Asian] individuality is not a virtue but a defect. So it is in the realm of communicative purpose. . . . The needs of the community take definite precedence over those of any individual. . . . In short, a speaker was not to devise but to discover the proper purpose for a speech; and when found it would be not so much his own as that of his group. The focal point . . . would not be *my purpose* but *our purpose* . . . which had far-reaching effects in the whole range of Asian principles and strategies. [Oliver, 1971:268]

This "my purpose/our purpose" distinction is developed more fully in Chapter 3, where a distinction is developed between individual purpose in an authority dyad and mutual purpose in an interchange dyad.

To describe the function of purpose in human communication most easily, it is necessary to assume the role of system observer or people-watcher. Suppose you find a comfortable chair in any airport in the world. You observe two men meet, shake hands, converse intently, shake hands again, and go their separate ways. At Orly Airport in Paris, the handshakes would be brief and vigorous; at Kennedy Airport in New York, the handshake might be longer and less vigorous; at Haneda in Tokyo, a bow would replace the handshake, and so on. In these cases, you observe a very decisive beginning and ending point to communication. You correctly observe that the men agree on when to start and when to stop. Many auto accidents, by the way, occur because of a lack of similar agreement. So the start/stop signals are important in communication.

If you move a bit closer to the next dyad you observe, you will notice that the two communicators both seem to be listening all the time, and they alternate speaking time. Only 4 or 5 percent of the time do they both talk at the same time, and then only briefly. You conclude that they switch speaker roles in what appears to be a planned way.

If you observe the next dyad even more closely, you may notice that occasionally one communicator repeats what he has just said with a slight variation. He corrects himself. At other times, one communicator asks a brief question and the other revises or elaborates what he has just said. You observe that there seems to be a fair amount of moment-by-moment change and adaptation within the system. If the two communicators are from different cultures, it is likely that these little subroutines may take 20 to 50 percent of the total talking time.

The three sample observations are taken as the sufficient and necessary evidence for purpose within a system. The communicators agree on a starting and stopping time. The communicators switch back and forth smoothly. The communicators revise and elaborate as they proceed, as required by their purpose. Without a specifiable purpose, one cannot even detect an "error." As a minimum, then, a system is purposeful in its operation when its various parts start and stop simultaneously, when internal activity is smoothly coordinated, and when error deviations are detected and corrected as they occur.

Communication systems operate within a communication network to achieve some purpose. In general, the more specific the purpose for communication, the more likely the communicators are to achieve their purpose. If they are unable to achieve their purpose, they will discover that fact at an early moment.

A word of caution should be added at this point. It is not always possible to achieve a purpose. The expectations which a communicator has for success in intercultural communication must be somewhat different. We shall examine this matter in several units in the later chapter (Oliver, 1971:268).

WORLDVIEW

In the preceding units, some of the components necessary to form a worldview of human communication have been sketched. Other necessary parts of the whole will be added as we go along.

The term "worldview" is the best one available now, but it is not fully adequate for our purposes. First of all, it refers to a single sense, to viewing, rather than to a multisensory "view" of the world. What each of us knows of the world depends on our eyes, ears, nose, and the other sensors as well. "World sense" is a more descriptive but awkward term (Ong in Prosser, 1973:27).

We *construct* our sense of the world and the place of man as communicator in the scheme of world things. Some microcultures seem to have no worldview. To some extent, the concept seems to depend on technology, in particular, communication technology. And among those communicators that do develop or discover or construct a worldview, it must be anticipated that such a worldview is influenced by the microculture of the home community of each of those communicators (Burton, 1972).

When we wish to look at the whole world, it is necessary to introduce a few additional new concepts. One of these is *biosphere* and another is *communication space.* The biosphere extends below sea level to about 35,000 feet and extends above the mountaintops to about 35,000 feet. More than 95 percent of the life on earth lives in the region between sea level and 10,000 feet above sea level. The most heavily used communication space falls in the same region. However, the geostationary communication satellite is parked at 22,300 miles above the equator, and that device increases human communication space. Space travel to the moon and beyond further extends communication space. For the present, it is adequate for us to view communication space as coinciding with the biosphere.

The world we view has a surface of 197 million square miles. Fifty-seven million square miles are land, and the remaining 140 million square miles are water. The 3.6 billion of us are distributed unequally over the land surface, with large numbers clustered in the megalopolis of Tokyo, New York, and other world centers (McHale, 1972).

The two world communication networks link the inhabitants of earth together. Some say we are now members of a global village. More exactly, each of us who develops a worldview is a member of the global world and a local village. For many economic and educational purposes, we are world citizens. For many social and cultural purposes, we are home community citizens. The fact that we can be both the global man and the village man should not lead us to conclude that we are global village men. We shall return to this notion from time to time, because it is a critical one in the study of intercultural communication. Increasingly, we live in a two-level culture, and a central task for the communicator is to shift from one level to the other (Bohannan, 1972:40).

DEVELOPMENTAL STAGES

The human communicator develops and maintains his communication skills in his home community. Stage by stage he further develops or enlarges his communication skills. A first major step is into the intercommunity level; from the intercommunity level, he may evolve into the international level; and from the international level, he may evolve into the world level. After the world level, or as a part of it, he may evolve skills necessary for human–animal, man–machine and man–ETI (Extra Terrestrial Intelligence) communication. These relationships are shown in Figure 4.

To an extent, the divisions shown in Figure 4 are arbitrary. The cultural differences between any two communicators could more accurately be represented on a continuum. But the experience of many communicators and the research relevant to intercultural communication tend to encourage such groupings, and they do provide a convenient emphasis for the last four chapters. The stages shown in Figure 4 should be viewed with an appropriate skepticism.

IN ADDITION

Browse through the Bibliography. A number of books listed there elaborate on the content of this chapter. In particular, examine Cherry, *World Communication*; Burton, *World Society*; Prosser, *Intercommunication Among Nations and Peoples*; and *From Semaphore to Satellite*, published by the International Telecommunica-

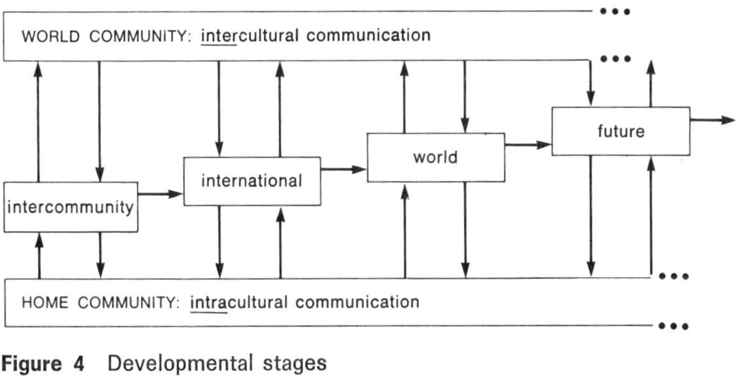

Figure 4 Developmental stages

tion Union. In addition, journals such as *Telecommunication, Aviation,* and *Journal of Communication* contain articles that provide specific information about the content of the various chapter units. Finally, my book, *Human Communication*, contains a fuller development of the concepts presented in this chapter.

Examine carefully the *Universal Declaration of Human Rights* which is reprinted in full on pages 127–132. Read all 30 articles; examine Articles 19 and 20 carefully. How many of these articles require communication for their realization? How many require intercultural communication?

Also, examine the Student Projects on pages 137–152. These projects are an integral part of the book. Are you most attracted to a Specialization Alternative, a Generalization Alternative, or a Third Alternative you invent for yourself?

2

Culture and Communication

In the previous chapter, a worldview of communication was developed. Chapter units were devoted to change, world communication revolutions, world communication networks, communication systems, and the concept of purpose.

In this chapter, the special relationship between culture and communication will be examined in some detail. Definitions of culture and of communication are provided. The similarities and differences between home community and world community are discussed. Intercultural communication is distinguished from cross-cultural communication. A description of a cultural mosaic is provided. The technological aspects of the two communication networks are examined again.

The next chapter is devoted to intercultural interchange.

INTRODUCTION

The two world communication networks remove constraints on human choice. The telecomnet of telephone–satellite–telephone components makes it possible for two men to interchange information across the cultural boundaries of their respective home communities, while each remains in the comfortable environment of his home. The transcomnet of auto–airplane–auto components makes it possible for one man to travel from his home community to the home community of any other man and there engage in the interchange of information. To be sure, as you read this, constraints on telecommunication and transportation do continue to exist for the majority of us who share the resources of the planet earth. These constraints are of four basic types: lack of communication facilities, existing rules and regulations, present attitudes toward communication, and level of communication skill. Fortunately, together we can reduce any or all of these constraints. We shall examine how these four constraints might be reduced, while keeping in focus the question, What will the future consequences be?

Lack of Communication Facilities

The term *communication facilities* refers to the technology, the hardware, required by the two world communication networks. For our purposes, it is sufficient to consider cars and planes, and telephones and satellites. These items cost substantial sums to acquire, and require additional sums for maintenance. The question arises, Who pays for what?

Today, all nations, but not all communities, have telephone facilities. Throughout Intelsat—the International Satellite Consortium—most nations have access to one or more satellites for their international telephone traffic.

The world telecomnet clearly exists. But its links are not evenly distributed on the basis of population. As in the use of most other resources, the United States, with 5 percent of the world's population, utilizes a much higher percentage of the world's physical resources.

The industrial capacity of the developed countries of the world is more than adequate for the manufacture of the required technological items. What is required is a means of distribution. Up to now, the United Nations has not been notably successful in stimulating this type of distribution.

The satellite project in India, for instance, is for direct television broadcast from a central ministry of education to the village communities. There will be one TV set per village to provide a "window to the world." Even though the objectives of such endeavor are admirable and the project in total may, by the year 2000, be shown to have beneficial consequences, such a one-way broadcast project is in no way a substitute for the type of two-way intercultural communication which is our concern here.

The fears and hatreds that lead to war are less likely to emerge when peoples and nations are in regular contact with each other. Several independent research projects support this assertion. In the broad sense of national defense, it becomes reasonable to allocate funds to constructive communication facilities instead of destructive engines of war. If the major countries were to allocate as little as 10 percent of their present annual defense budgets to the improvement of world communication facilities, within a very few years the constraints which now exist would be removed. Those of us who live in the developed countries would come to feel more secure with an airport than with a missile site, with a 707 than with an F-111, or a Concorde rather than a Mig, with a passenger bus rather than a military truck, with a communication satellite rather than a spy satellite, with civilian telephone facilities rather than military communications equipment, and so on.

In addition, support for a gradual decrease in the cost of using the desired facilities to the point of their being totally free would be required. National defense is now supported by tax monies. Communication facilities, as an enlightened form of world defense, might be also. At present, most large businesses find it economically sound to provide telephone and travel support for their employees. On a larger scale, research shows a strong relationship between the development of communication facilities and a country's economic development. Why not, then, make it a first priority to provide all men with free and full use of communication facilities at the earliest possible time (Lerner and Schramm, 1967)?

Existing Rules and Regulations

The world communication networks are regulated by two major United Nations agencies: the International Telecommunication Union in Geneva (ITU) and the International Civil Aviation Organization (ICAO) in Montreal. The rules and regulations, at the world level, are under continual study, and every few years major conferences are held to review and revise the regulations. In broad terms, the mechanism exists for evolving a satisfactory world order in the use of communication facilities (Alexandrowicz, 1971).

The situation at the national level is quite different. The national rules and regulations for communication policy are closely related to government policy. An outside observer might label such policies as censorship, promulgation of the party line, serving the interests of business at the expense of the public, and so on. Within the larger national culture, the particular rules and regulations make cultural "sense," even though they quite often restrict intercultural communication at the intercommunity, international, and world levels.

As a traveler, it is quite easy to find points to criticize in the regulation of communication within any nation. It is a sobering task to propose an alternate set of regulations which would, in the future, constitute an improvement. For instance, present United States communication regulations result in the "mass media" display of violence as a device for selling commercial products. It is quite easy to criticize such a state of affairs; research shows the negative influence of such programming. Yet, workable alternatives that are culturally acceptable have yet to be proposed. Why?

Attitudes Toward Communication

Attitudes toward "talking to strangers" vary from community to community and nation to nation. To be sure, there is substantial variation within a community and within a person, from time to time. In general, the formation of any group results in a group being for certain things and against others. The more "tightly knit" a community is, the more specialized its members will be to the requirements of that community, and the less time they will spend communicating with others from outside that community. The Amish communities in the United States mainland provide an example of communication contained mostly within the community. Rather little is with others outside the community, except for specific purposes related to work outside the community. Another example, and a more extreme one, is found in the island community of Niihau in the Hawaiian Island chain. In Niihau, the early Hawaiian culture is preserved, access to the island is by boat only, and permission must be secured to come ashore. Few outsiders enter the community, and few who live there travel outside it. Recently, small communities of "Stone Age" men have been found in the mountain areas of the remote islands of the Philippine chain. As outsiders, should we *promote* community sanctuaries to preserve these cultures? Certainly an increase in communication with the outsiders will change things.

Those persons who live and work in the center of the large cities present a marked contrast. During the course of a day, they may communicate almost entirely with persons from around the world that they have not seen before and do not expect to see again. The international airport areas with gift shops, airline ticket counters, and related services are characterized by communication for very limited purposes that operates in a routine way regardless of the country or the language used.

Somewhere between the community which isolates itself almost totally from the outside world and the community which interacts so intensively with other parts of the world that it is hard to recognize it as a community, the *appropriate* mix of intracommunity and intercultural communication will be discovered. As yet, helpful guidelines do not exist.

Communication Skill

The communication skills developed in a home community provide a base for future intercultural communication at the intercommunity, international, and world levels. But these community-developed skills are only a first step. The adult who regularly walks to a neighbor's home to converse with him may be bewildered by his first walk-through of the procedures preceding an international air flight. Equally, the adult who may for years carry on conversations with his neighbor across the back fence will, when he places his first international phone call, raise his voice, and he may forget what he wanted to say.

In finer detail, the second-by-second interchange in intercultural communication requires a great deal of revision and elaboration as communication proceeds, if the purpose is to be achieved. If you listen in on an intercultural dyad organized by two persons with very little communication experience outside their home communities, you will notice a higher frequency of phrases such as, "What did you say?" "I thought you said ______." "You mean you don't have ______?" "You honestly don't believe ______?" And so on. These little "revise and elaboration" sequences require time and tend to interrupt the flow of communication. Most importantly, they are extremely important individual and cultural differences in the number of times it is "polite" to ask another person to repeat a word, or explain something again. You can test this very simply on your friends and on strangers from another culture. The critical point is that if two communicators do not command sufficient skill to maintain the revise/elaborate correction procedures within culturally acceptable limits, they will *inescapably* introduce error and confusion severe enough to result in the termination of communication. When that happens, the problem is seldom detected by the communicators who have experienced it. Too often, they conclude that the "______" are really not worth talking to after all.

Communication skill requirements differ at several levels. Seldom is the specialization acquired in a home community effective, without some modification, in intercommunity communication, even though it provides the essential base. One does not expect that being able to write by hand enables him to type, even though it helps quite a bit. There are typewriting training programs. There are few comparable training programs that identify the training objective as facilitating intercommunity communication. More often, such programs are usually described as teaching correct pronunciation or removing the *dis* from disadvantaged communication. The problem is much the same for the student who learns a language in a classroom from a teacher who also learned the language in a classroom. These points will be further elaborated in the later chapters.

The four constraints on intercultural communication—lack of facilities, regulations, attitudes and skills—are strongly interrelated. More importantly, they are each in their own way expressions of culture at the community, national, and world levels.

SOME DEFINITIONS OF CULTURE AND COMMUNICATION

Both culture and communication are woven into the fabric of the human condition. Not surprisingly, almost everyone who develops a serious interest, sooner, rather than later, attempts to specify what he means by the term culture, or the term communication, or, as in our case, intercultural communication. Definitions abound. The task here is to sort from among a few likely definitional statements those few most appropriate to our task, and to fashion from those few one statement on which we might agree. For these few pages will be our touchstone, or benchmark, or working definition.

There are two predefinitional statements on which wide agreement exists today:

The cultural background of a communicator influences almost every detail and every pattern of his communication activities.

Communication between communicators of similar cultural background is usually easier, more reliable, faster, safer, etc., than is communication between communicators of dissimilar cultural backgrounds.

On most other matters that are included within the core of interests that form the topic areas of intercultural communication, there are alternate viewpoints. An acquaintance with this diversity can sharpen our understanding and practice. Let us look, then, at some definitions of culture.

Culture Defined Somewhat

A first place to look for a definition is a dictionary:

> . . . a particular form or stage of civilization, as that of a certain nation or period: Greek culture; the sum total of ways of living built up by a group of human beings and transmitted from one generation to another. [*Random House Dictionary*, 1966:353]

Obviously such a definition is so broad it includes almost everything and does not exclude enough. A first task of a good definition is to help determine where a thing begins and where it ends; in short, to be able to recognize "one" where it is seen.

Arensberg and Niehoff define culture thusly:

> Culture is the sum total of what individuals learn in common with other members of the group to which they belong. Basically, it is what an individual has learned from the people who reared him, most of which they learned from their elders. Cultural knowledge also includes what the individual learns from his fellows and from his teachers when they formally or informally pass on group knowledge. [Arensberg and Niehoff, 1971:16]

Karl Deutsch defines culture in this way:

> . . . culture [is] based on the community of communication, consisting of socially stereotyped patterns of behavior, including habits of language and thought, and carried on through various forms of social learning, particularly through methods of child rearing standardized in this culture. [Deutsch, 1966:37]

Note in this definition of culture the central relationship between culture and communication.

René Dubos makes a related observation:

> . . . clearly culture, if this word is defined as everything learned by experience and transmitted from one generation to the next, can reach high levels without elaborate technology. Culture is the expression of man's responses to the physical and human environment. These responses take the form of behavioral patterns and emotional relationships as well as the development of utilitarian objects. [Dubos, 1968:38]

But Dubos makes a vital counterpoint: Each human being is unique, unprecedented, and unrepeatable (Dubos, 1968:vii).

For all the shaping power of a culture, and that power is considerable, each person remains to some degree unique in the way he walks and talks. On the phone, we can recognize a friend's voice almost instantly, and we can recognize his footsteps when he walks in a hall. Cultural forces differ most, perhaps, in whether they move to develop the unique characteristics of an *individual* or whether they encourage the social characteristics of the cultural *group.*

Culture, at this point in the discussion, consists of the learning acquired by the members of a group in the process of living as they live. It can be recognized by consistent or stereotyped patterns of behaving. It is transmitted from generation to generation by habits of child rearing. In the past, cultures have evolved slowly over time.

Margaret Mead recently drew attention to the acceleration of change in the cultures of the many communities of the world. She distinguishes three types of culture-shaping patterns.

Postfigurative—in which the grandparent holding a new grandchild in his arms can imagine no future for that child other than the patterns of his own life. The postfigurative pattern has been the dominant one in all of the traditional communities of the world and in *all* communities up to at least 1800. This postfigurative pattern of culture formation shaped the most deeply held and often unspeakable convictions that most of us still hold today. The postfigurative is pretechnological.

Cofigurative—in which the parent sends his children to school, where he learns from his teachers and his peers the elements of a culture only partially known by the parents.

Prefigurative—in which the newborn child becomes the symbol of what is to come, and a task of cultures becomes that of supporting a child in whatever direction his future leads him. In such a culture, persons of all ages recognize that they are equally ignorant of what is to come in the near and distant future (Mead, 1970).

In a prefigurative culture, change is rapid. Mead considers that we are now moving into a prefigurative era. In such a context, the culture of a home community and a nation are likely to undergo an accelerated reshaping. The principal force behind such cultural reshaping is communication as facilitated by the two world networks.

In recent years, UNESCO has initiated a series of studies on cultural policy. These studies are to identify the human needs for culture, to specify the cultural needs of man, and, in general, to evolve statements of cultural policy (Cultural Policy, 1969).

Communication Defined Somewhat

Below is a dictionary definition of communication:

> Act or process of communicating, fact of being communicated; the imparting or interchange of thoughts, opinions, or information by speech, writing, or signs; something imparted, interchanged or transmitted; a document or message imparting news, views, information, etc.; passage, or an opportunity or means of passage, between places. [*Random House Dictionary*, 1966:298]

Again, as in the case of culture, the dictionary definition is broad and inclusive.

In a recent book of readings on communication theory, Sereno and Mortensen define communication in this way:

> The term "communication" may be defined as a *process by which senders and receivers of messages interact in given social contexts.* [Sereno and Mortensen, 1970:5]

Rogers employs the following definition:

> Communication is the process by which messages are transferred from a source to a receiver. [Rogers, 1971:11]

Cherry states:

> Strictly, the word communication comes from the Latin *communico*—meaning share. *Share*, notice, not "I send messages." Communication is essentially a social process. [Cherry, 1971:2]

In an examination of a hundred published definitions of communication, Dance found that these definitions differed most on three points: level of *observation*, presence or absence of *intent* or purpose, and presence or absence of judgments of *success* or goodness (Dance, 1970:201). When there is lack of consensus on the rather dull matter of definition, it usually suggests that "additional research" is required to clarify that matter. I take this to be the case with both communication and culture at the present time. Needless to say, the definitional problem is confounded and compounded in the case of intercultural communication.

Intercultural Communication Delineated

In this book, our concern is with communication between human communicators of dissimilar cultural backgrounds. In particular, our primary interest is in that two-way communication of the type called intercultural interchange. Such communication can always be viewed as occurring in one of the two world networks, and in one of two communication systems:

Intercultural communication occurs in either a dyadic or small group communication system operating for some mutual purpose within either the telecomnet or the transcomnet.

The large group system is excluded because it seldom operates as a two-way system or for a mutual purpose. Excluding the large group leaves exactly four possibilities:

Dyadic system/telecomnet, as in a telephone conversation
Dyadic system/telecomnet, as in a face-to-face dialog
Small group system/telecomnet, as in a conference call
Small group system/transcomnet, as in a committee meeting

We have now delineated the area of intercultural communication to a size that can be treated in a small book. The concept of intercultural interchange as a fundamental pattern of communication will be further expanded in the next chapter.

The proposed delineation or outline of intercultural communication employed in this book differs in either *observability*, *intent*, or *success* from other such statements currently proposed for intercultural communication. For instance:

Men must communicate, whether or not they will communicate. [Prosser, 1973:1]

. . . intercultural communication can best be understood as cultural variance in the perception of social objects and events. The barriers to communication caused by this perceptual variance can best be lowered by a knowledge and understanding of cultural factors that are subject to variance, coupled with an honest and sincere desire to communicate successfully across cultural boundaries. [Porter in Samovar and Porter, 1972:5]

Intercultural communication . . . involves communicator and audience of entirely different to slightly different cultures. [Sitaram in Samovar and Porter, 1972:23]

Culture is a code we learn and share, and learning and sharing require communication. And communication requires coding and symbols, which must be learned and shared. Communication and culture are inseparable. [Smith, 1966:7]

At this time, intercultural communication is viewed somewhat differently by those of us who are most interested in it. I take this to be a healthy state of the science and art!

HOME COMMUNITY

There are a very large number of communities in the world today that meet the usual tests for a community. Such communities are called villages, settlements, towns, and a variety of other names. They range in size from a few hundred to a few thousand inhabitants. At times they are separated from other nearby communities by uninhabited land, coastlines, mountains, or rivers. But not all communities have natural boundaries. Communities sometimes exist within cities and are bounded by railroad tracks, wide streets, and, most effectively, invisible territorial lines that exist, as do so many things, on the basis of a maintained common consent.

The essential feature of a community is that it has a center. Such a center may have a cluster of homes and shops and a town hall or post office or bus station. Or it may depend on other less tangible features for its core. The important thing is that the people who live in the community agree that there is a center and know where it is. "How do I get to the center of town?" is a question the traveler can get answered consistently in a small community (Buber, 1969:87).

How far the community extends outward from the center is a much more difficult question both for resident and for the technical description of a community. Fortunately, it need not concern us here.

For our purposes, it is enough to be able to ask a person where his home is and in what community his home is located. His answer supplies information sufficiently exact for us to examine the communication facilities available to him, the rules and regulations that apply to his communication activities, the dominant attitudes in his immediate community toward intercultural communication, and the level of skill developed in intercultural communication. We can roughly determine the surface distance between that person's home and any other person's home. Further, if we know either the person's annual income or the average income for his community, we can begin to estimate his use of communication facilities and his degree of involvement in intercultural communication (Bagdikian, 1971).

As you know from your own experience, communities differ markedly from one another in certain respects and appear quite similar in others. As Dubos pointed out, each individual human is unique and unprecedented. In the same sense, that statement can be applied to a community. Each home community is unique and unprecedented. The degree of uniqueness depends on a number of factors—which are important to both culture and communication.

The first factor stems from the interplay of community boundaries and mobility. A community with well-defined boundaries and a stable population, particularly if it is an older community, will become organized. There will be elected or self-selected leaders, community ordinances, a cluster of attitudes, and a variety of skills. In short, an inherited culture will be preserved and transmitted, and in that process it will be changed a little to accommodate changes stimulated from other sources.

An organized community will reveal a second factor of social stratification. There will be at least two social classes: the elite and the masses, or more simply, the "haves" and the "have nots." If these categories are not rigid, a third level or middle class may evolve. Even in a quiet traditional home community, a certain amount of cultural change does occur. But it may well be imperceptible during a single life span.

Within a traditional home community, the basic communication patterns are quite well understood. There is more intraclass communication than there is interclass communication. A member of a higher class may engage a member of a lower class in communication whenever he wishes, but the reverse is not true, thereby creating a downward flow of information. If a visitor enters the community, he is immediately taken to the community chief. The chief talks to the visitor, and may or may not permit the visitor to talk to other community members. If the community has one radio, it will be in the chief's home. He will decide what others may listen to, or listen himself and report to others what is "good" for them to know. And so on. Information flows into the community at the top and may or may not flow down to the other members of that community. An effective control of information makes it possible to maintain the cultural traditions of a community.

Even in a modern community, the same basic processes are at work. Community leaders receive special briefings and, in general, both seek and receive more information related to the affairs of the total community than do the nonleaders. Further, the patterns of "within" and "between" class communication are discernible.

Some years ago, Leonard Bloomfield coined the term *speech community.* A speech community, as he described it, resembles the ensemble of humans we are calling a home community. A speech community reveals a set of consistent patterns in the speech of the community members. An outsider might assert that all members of that community speak a peculiar dialect. The community members themselves would distinguish at least two and perhaps three levels of speech. Listening to tape recordings of voices, they could very accurately state whether the speakers were of high, middle, or low class. A high degree of communicative interaction within a community will lead to a *specialized* style of communicating that an outside observer might call a dialect.

The patterns of interaction within a community are influenced by social class. Social class leads to at least two and usually three or more distinct substyles that are quickly and accurately recognized by all members of that community. As we shall see, strong cultural values are embedded in these distinctions. While such matters of style may pass with little awareness within the community itself, they often become of dramatic importance when a community member first attempts to engage in intercultural communication at the intercommunity level (Bloomfield, 1933).

WORLD COMMUNITY

The question is, Do we now have a single world community, a single world culture? There are a variety of answers to that question. For the sake of simplicity, let us take two responses, one yes, one no, and examine them briefly. Marshall McLuhan of Toronto says *yes*, that the networks of communication make all of us inhabitants of a single global village. Colin Cherry of London says *no*, that the world is not my village. At best, I can hope to know my family, have half a dozen friends, and get to know a hundred or so people fairly well. My village is small and cut to the human dimension. Hajime Nakamura of Tokyo observes that there is much talk about our being members of one world, but that our repeated stress on this particular point suggests we have yet to accept that transformation with any degree of comfort.

There are many developments that encourage a one-world view. The two world communication networks are a first example. Many major problems are transnational: population growth and pollution control, to mention but two obvious ones. Further, there has been a dramatic growth in world organizations. More than 2,500 major international organizations involved in business, government, education, and other fields now operate routinely. The United Nations has existed for more than a quarter century and continues to work in a wide range of fields. The list can be very long.

The "newsworthy" happenings in any community of the world are known by at least some members of a vast majority of the world communities within minutes after they have happened, or more frequently now, as they are happening. The moon walk–talk by the Apollo 11 crew is perhaps the most dramatic example. In the past, one important characteristic of a community was that its members were similarly informed. In the sense of an increasing quantity of shared information, we are becoming members of a single global village. In a few years, direct satellite-to-home TV broadcasting will be possible on a worldwide scale on a routine basis. Such a development will further increase the actual or potential store of shared information among all the people of the world.

On the other hand, there are developments that encourage us to consider that the direction will be toward a world of many diverse but interdependent communities. One strong sign of this is the failure of the American "melting pot" to produce a uniform American. Similar failures can be observed elsewhere, as in Switzerland or Canada. There is an unexpected strength in the grass-roots cultural base of the home community. Somehow, it manages to maintain some distinctive cultural patterns in the face of pressures from educational systems and mass media. Bill

Moyers, in his journey across America, catches the flavor of some of these community enclaves (Moyers, 1971).

When contrasted with the smaller village community, the nation state is a very new invention of man. The small communities have endured for thousands upon thousands of years. The present nation states are 200 or fewer years old.

The small home community permits man to develop and maintain a wide variety of associations. First, through intimate daily communication, man forms and maintains a family. He forms a few close friendships. And he forms a large network of cooperative community-based associations.

Those who look to one world point to the increased opportunities available for processing information. Those who look to the home community proclaim the importance of association, of strong interpersonal relationships, of good, old friends. The quest for information soon leads any community member out of his community and into the large world. The quest for a full range of human relationships pulls him toward the small community. Nowhere more than in intercultural communication is a delicate balance between information and association required. Terms such as culture-shock, underdevelopment, communication barriers, stagnation, and communication overload label the problems that arise at unexpected moments. Oversimply, the seeking of information of vital importance to the concerns of the individual communicator and his community leads on to the formation of new associations that may, at times, be extremely uncomfortable. Inescapably, intercultural communication encompasses both information processing and human association, or, in brief, intercultural interchange.

INTERCULTURAL AND CROSS-CULTURAL

When employed informally, the terms intercultural and cross-cultural are often used interchangeably. For our purposes, it is necessary to make a simple distinction. The term intercultural is appropriate for our discussion, while the term cross-cultural is not.

Dubos' point that each human is in some sense "unique and unrepeatable" provides a starting point for a distinction between intercultural and cross-cultural. Any individual assimilates the culture of his home community, but he does so imperfectly and incompletely. We have largely given up the search for the "average man." We must not also expect to find a culture faithfully embodied in a single man.

A student of culture will observe a community group for long periods, noting the behavior of individuals, but more importantly, recording the patterns of interaction across a wide range of human activities, a range both larger than and somewhat different from our concerns for the purposes of communication. Detailed studies of two or more cultures may be compared and contrasted. A *cross-cultural* study may be performed. The term cross-cultural is reserved, then, for the systematic comparison of two or more cultures. See Figure 5.

From this viewpoint, cross-cultural communication is engaged in by diplomats and government leaders speaking to their counterparts in an official capacity. Summit meetings and other "high-level" talks are good examples of cross-cultural communication. It occurs when the culturally sanctioned office of the president of the United States communicates with the culturally sanctioned office of the chairman of the People's Republic of China. Such communication may continue long after the present officeholders remain in office.

When mass media of radio and television are used to further national and international interests, they are instruments of cross-cultural communication. Government leaders inform their respective publics of action taken via mass media. Significantly,

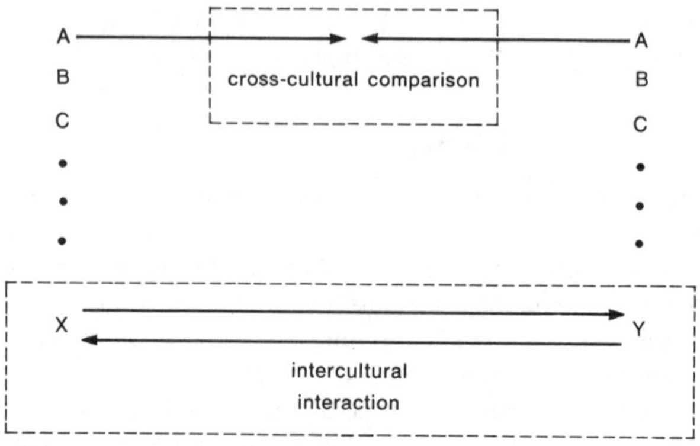

Figure 5 Comparing cross-cultural and intercultural communication

mass media—the large group system in the telecomnet—are most effective as disseminators of information and supporters of existing cultural attitudes and associations. They are quite ineffective as a means for changing basic cultural values. In general, the messages of cross-cultural communication originate in "high places" and are transmitted via large one-way systems to the members of the various communities (Prosser, 1973).

Intercultural communication is participant communication. It occurs between a member of one community and a member of another community. These communities may be near or distant from each other. Or, intercultural communication may occur among a small group of communicators from two or more culturally different communities. In either the dyad or small group, intercultural communication is characterized by intense involvement on the part of the participant communicators.

Intercultural communication is two-way communication. The participants exchange information and form unique associations or relationships; in a word, they engage in intercultural *interchange.* More exactly, intercultural communication occurs in either a dyadic or small group communication system. Such a system is organized to achieve a mutual purpose. It may operate in either a telecomnet or a transcomnet.

More broadly, intercultural communication and cross-cultural communication may be distinguished by the following general tendencies:

Intercultural communication	*Cross-cultural communication*
Two-way	One-way
Dyadic, small group	Large group
Mutual purpose	Individual purpose
Unofficial	Official
Informal	Formal
Developed message	Prepared message
Interdependent	Hierarchial

Other distinctions will occur to you as we proceed.

There is a final point to be raised. Intercultural communication has a time tag attached to it. For instance, through the intercultural interchange, any two culturally dissimilar persons activate the process that forms a culture. Together, out of their communication, they build a new dyadic subculture. It will be a small thing, perhaps, but it can meet many of the tests for a culture. The questions before us are:

Does such subculture building lead on to a single world culture?
Does it lead on to even more diversity in cultures than we have at present?
Can both one world culture and many diverse community cultures exist at the same time?
What will be the likely long-term consequences of "intercultural" man–machine communication?

CULTURAL MOSAIC

A mosaic is a pattern that depends both on the arrangement of dots on a surface and on the viewer's manner of examining it. In other words, like many cultural matters, a mosaic pattern is partly determined by a configuration of dots and partly determined by what the viewer expects to see. For the purposes of intercultural communication, it is necessary to imagine a very large, three-dimensional mosaic that enables us to view spatial patterns on one surface and time patterns on another.

Our three-dimensional time/space mosaic has 3.6 billion dots, each of which is both unique—in the sense that each human is unique—and shows patterns of similarity, as members of a family and a community do. Obviously, it would be troublesome to draw or build such a mosaic, but I suspect you can build one within the "theatre of your mind." Think about it.

Now that you have created the mosaic, look first at the overall pattern. The dominant pattern you observe is that human dots with similar cultural characteristics tend to cluster together. A closer examination reveals that some dots are totally of one type and others show a blend of characteristics. The dots are not evenly spaced across space, but tend to form communitylike clusters. Further, in some areas there are many more clusters of dots than there are in other areas. As you ponder the arrangement of human dots across space, you will from time to time observe other patterns.

Turning the mosaic to the time dimension, the first thing that impresses you is that the number of dots has significantly increased in the last 200 years. The projections for one alternative future show as many as 6 billion dots by the year 2000. Over the 200-year time span, you observe incredible migrations to areas of the mosaic where few dots had existed before. And the shape and size of the configurations also change over time. Finally, a closer look at the individual dots shows that while most of them move about in a relatively small area, others at times move over vast regions in relatively short times. In recent times, a new kind of linkage between widely separated dots becomes evident. In sum, there seems to be a more rapid change in many of the dots in relatively short periods of time than has ever been observed before.

The mosaic device may be awkward for you to work with. You may wish to use a moving picture that can be stopped and examined frame by frame. Or you may prefer Buckminster Fuller's 200-foot, computer-operated, and floatable model of the world. In any case, for most of us, some artificial device helps us to move conceptually from an intercultural dyad in the here and now to the whole of mankind—past, present and future (Fuller, 1969:157).

It takes a very large framework in which to pose the questions:

What is the best balance between intracultural and intercultural communication?
Might such a balance differ from decade to decade in a human life?
In the case of intercultural communication, are the dangers of information overload minor or serious?
Will large-scale intercultural communication strengthen or destroy existing cultures?

And so on.

COMMUNICATION NETWORKS AGAIN

The two world communication networks are called the telecomnet and the transcomnet. The telecomnet includes the telephone and the communication satellite, while the transcomnet includes the automobile and the airplane. In each of these networks, one major component is missing.

This missing component is the required "ground station." Such ground stations are located within the home community. The telecomnet ground station includes a telephone exchange for local and long-distance calls and the additional components required to link that exchange to the satellite for long-distance calls. The transcomnet ground station includes the local airport and the highways that lead to it. The similarities of function of the telecomnet and transcomnet ground stations are quite striking.

Communities have always been strongly influenced by the structure of their communication facilities. At the moment, there are quite a number of technological developments at the tryout stage or the early implementation stage. The *cable* which can bring into the home an equivalent of forty or more two-way telephone lines is being installed in some communities. In others, neighborhood heliports and other innovations in home-to-airport transportation are being put into operation. The technological developments in both networks are now very rapid and promise to accelerate in the future.

Both networks now have a feature that has far-reaching implications for intercultural communication. The capacity of both networks is *allocable* rather than fixed.

In the telecomnet, the capacity of the satellite can be allocated *as needed* among a wide number of ground stations in a large number of communities. The transoceanic telephone cable could provide telephone service only between major population centers. There are still communities in the world that have either no telephone service or no reliable telephone service because of the difficulty in stringing lines or laying cable and because of the difficulty of keeping such equipment in working order, once it has been installed. The *allocable* capacity of the satellite, along with its "wireless" characteristics, changes all of that. In the next few years, the impact of the allocable capacity on intercultural communication will be substantial.

In the transcomnet, the capacity of the jet plane can be allocated *as needed* among a wide number of ground stations in a large number of communities. Unlike the train, the jet can change its routes, or reallocate its capacity. Charter flights, excursion fares, and other alternatives are also available. While many smaller communities do not have airports, a bus station with bus service to a neighboring airport serves, though not as well. The growth of long-distance air travel has been both recent and dramatic. Again, the impact of intercultural communication promises to be substantial.

The world is still some 8,000 miles in diameter. It has not shrunk. But in terms of the pretechnological walk–talk distance, the time it takes a human to traverse a given amount of space has shrunk. Telephone communication between many communities can be nearly instantaneous. While Phileas Fogg went around the earth in eighty days, a spaceship orbits it in ninety minutes. Even with conventional aircraft, no two earth communities are more than one man-day apart.

The two world communication networks are now developed fully enough to permit us to consider a day, not far in the future, when any one of us who inhabits this planet may, if he chooses, communicate with any other one of us. In the evolution of the human brain, the billions of dotlike brain cells have gradually evolved an increasing number of interconnections. We are now able to conceive of the same thing happening among us who populate the world. The possibility exists for building a world intelligence from the linkages of the communities of the world, much as a community has an intelligence gleaned from that of its individual members. Such a global intelligence could cope with the problems of man on earth—resource utilization, population, pollution, and a dozen more. Beyond that, we could develop together the destiny that lays before us as we explore the stars. To bring a world intelligence, several billion strong, into being will require intercultural communication on a scale and of a quality not yet known on earth.

IN ADDITION

The Bibliography lists a variety of books that elaborate on the content of the various chapter units. Examine Mead, *Culture and Commitment*; Girard, *Cultural Development*; Arensberg and Niehoff, *Introducing Social Change*; Dubos, *So Human an Animal*; Samovar and Porter, *Intercultural Communication*; and Oliver, *Communication and Culture in Ancient India and China*. Look through other books "in the vicinity" of these in the bibliography, the bookstore, and the library. One finds useful information about intercultural communication in unexpected places; serendipity operates! Also, look at Alexandrowicz, *The Law of Global Communications*.

Study the *Declaration of the Principles of International Cultural Co-operation*, which is reprinted in full on pages 133–135. Do the *principles* constitute a complete and effective guide to a cultural policy that is *fair*, community by community, around the world? Will the development of strong local cultures in the many diverse home communities inhibit or facilitate intercultural communication?

3

Intercultural Interchange

In the previous two chapters, a worldview of human communication was outlined, and the relationship between communication and culture was examined.

In this chapter, separate units are devoted to the intercultural dyad, synergy and serendipity, and the right of man to communicate. Taken together, these units provide a description of intercultural interchange. This chapter completes the foundation materials for the study of intercultural communication.

The next chapter gets down to specific cases of intercultural communication at the intercommunity level and examines the problems and possibilities therein.

INTRODUCTION

Let us begin our discussion of intercultural interchange with a simple little problem that can be worked out on the back of an envelope. Assume a world with 100 communities evenly dispersed on the present land areas of the world. Each community has 100 members, making up a total world population of 10,000 persons. On the average, each community member engages in some type of communication for ten hours per day. To keep the matter simple, assume that nine of those hours are *intra*cultural communication within the community and of no immediate concern to us. The other one hour per day is intercultural communication. Such intercultural communication occurs only in dyads, equally divided between the telecomnet and the transcomnet. The distribution of distances is such that at least one out of every ten hours of intercultural communication links communicators from the most distant communities; the other nine of those ten hours utilize links of a variety of distances. For the purposes of intercultural communication on an average day, how many telephone channels and how many airline seats would be needed? Consider the effects of different time zones, flight speeds, and *other* related factors. What additional assumptions are needed to solve the problem? Can the solution be extended to the real world of 3.6 billion people?

While that little problem takes some scratching to solve, it does serve to introduce a basic question in the study of intercultural communication. How is it possible to be concerned with a single intercultural dyad, as an observer or a participant, and still retain a focus on the larger world of intercultural communication, of which this intercultural dyad and all other intercultural dyads are equally vital parts? Can we be interested in the trees, one by one, and the total forest? Can we be interested in the unique intercultural dyad and the worldwide consequences, for man and his cultures, of a major increase of intercultural communication? The framework that has been developed in the last two chapters may enable us to do so. In case there is any doubt, I should point out that it is not usually easy to keep the particular case and the general condition in focus at the same time. However, in intercultural communication it is especially important that we do so. The reasons for the importance of the particular and the general will become more apparent as we proceed.

INTERCULTURAL DYAD

A dyadic communication system is organized for some purpose by two communicators. When the two communicators are from different cultural backgrounds, the dyad is called an intercultural dyad. In general, the two participant communicators and a system observer will agree on whether a particular dyad is intercultural or is not intercultural. Most often, disagreement on this point occurs for fewer than 5 percent of the dyads. At any rate, we can safely discard from our discussion those dyadic systems in which there is disagreement. Whether or not a dyad is intercultural, then, rests on a specific decision by the persons most involved.

Like any other communication system, a dyad requires a minimum amount of organization to become an operating system. First, the communicators must agree when they commence communicating and when they cease communicating. Simple as this requirement appears to be, one observes instances in intercultural communication, some of them humorous and others tragic—as when a receiver clicks in the "middle" of a long-distance phone call—in which the simple start/stop cues are missed. Second, the communicators alternate as speakers. Of necessity, both communicators must listen all the time if they are to avoid "double talk," that is, having both talk at once. In most cases this is a relatively simple matter, but the alternating or switching cues vary from culture to culture. Communication systems can absorb only a very little "double talk," less than 10 percent usually, and continue to function smoothly. Third, the communicators must be able to revise and elaborate as they go along. The revision often involves the resaying of a word to make it more intelligible, or the restressing of a phrase. The elaboration usually involves supplying additional illustrative material or amplifying the original statement by other devices. If the revise/elaborate patterns do not operate smoothly, the flow of communication becomes snarled like a recording tape that breaks and runs off the reel. So, as a minimum, the two communicators must agree on the start/stop time for the system, they must coordinate the speaker switching, and they must revise/elaborate as they go along, as required by their purpose.

An intercultural dyad that meets the basic stop/start, switch/share, and revise/elaborate requirements may be said to be organized. It also demonstrates purpose. Even when purpose and organization exist, there is one additional matter of importance. An organized, purposeful system will display either an authority or interchange structure.

Authority Structure

An organized, purposeful intercultural dyad will be structured in one of two ways: as an intercultural authority dyad or as an intercultural interchange dyad. Interchange will be discussed in the next unit.

An authority structure emerges in a dyad when one of the two participating communicators performs, first of all, the basic organizing operations. The authority-communicator decides, by himself, when communication will start and stop. He determines speaker switching and time sharing; that is, he decides who says what, when it is said, and how much each communicator says. He also guides the revise/elaborate procedures. The authority-communicator determines what elements require revision and which ones require elaboration. In short, the authority-communicator controls communication.

The power of an authority-communicator also permits him to

determine the *purpose* of communication. Thus, an authority dyad as a communication system operates not for a *mutual* purpose, but for an individual purpose. An individual purpose can be fully determined prior to communication. Only rarely is the achievement of an individual purpose of equal consequence to both communicators.

The authority structure in a dyad leads to two basic message patterns. The first of these patterns is the tutorial; the second is the interview.

In the tutorial pattern, the authority becomes the tutor. He transmits information to the tutee. For the most part, he selects what he transmits and when to transmit it. Basically, the tutor as authority makes statements. From time to time, as part of a revise/elaborate sequence, he may ask the tutee questions. When he does so, he decides when to ask the question, what the question will be, and what is expected from the tutee as an answer. In a slightly less formal authority, the tutee may also ask questions, at times deemed appropriate by the tutor. But the tutor retains the privilege of answering or not answering a question, and he remains the final judge of what constitutes an answer.

It is instructive to observe a dyad operating in a strict tutorial plan. The patterns are so firmly established in most communities that they are seldom recognized as patterns that can be observed and described. Within every community, much of the cultural perspective is transmitted from one generation to the next in a tutorial pattern. The messages have been prepared over a very long time, often generations, and are to be received as guides to action and, in time, to be transmitted with only minor modification to the next generation. The *intra*cultural tutorial, then, is a major means of transmitting culture within a community.

The tutorial pattern, in which the tutor is the authority in charge of start/stop, switch/share, and revise/elaborate operations, extends quite naturally into other patterns. In particular, the large group systems in both the telecomnet and the transcomnet operate, almost entirely, in a tutorial pattern. The cofigurative culture transmission, discussed by Margaret Mead, passes part of the tutorial task to the classroom teacher and the mass media. When lecturing to a roomful of students, the classroom teacher acts as a tutor in all important ways. Likewise, the newsman "casts" new information onto the airways. The lecturer and the newsman are both tutors and, within a single community, serve to cofigure the culture.

In the interview pattern, the authority-communicator becomes the interviewer. He is quite free to determine individually the purpose of communication and to determine in advance what questions he will ask, and what he will accept as answers. In other words, he can prepare an "interview schedule" and develop criteria for determining when a question has been answered. Thus, in a manner similar to that of the tutorial, the interviewer controls the flow of communication in an intercultural dyad.

The interview can be seen as a specialization of the question-asking technique employed by a tutor. Like the tutor, the interviewer decides when a particular question is to be asked and when it has been answered to his satisfaction. An interesting mismatch often arises in the intercultural dyad structured on an authority basis. The authority-communicator who takes on the "burden" of controlling the intercultural dyad and regulating its performance often sees himself as being "helpful." He views his contribution as a positive one made at some sacrifice to himself. The other communicator in the dyad often sees the control and regulation activities as aggressive and dominating, inconsiderate and overbearing. While such opposite feelings of helpfulness and oppressiveness are not normally articulated within an intercultural dyad, they are frequently talked about within the respective home communities. Patterns of communication appropriate under certain circumstances within a community are unlikely to be appropriate in similar circumstances outside the community.

Interchange Structure

The interchange structure in the intercultural dyad is the heart of intercultural communication.

It would be difficult to overestimate the importance of intercultural interchange as a pattern of communication, both within a particular dyad and in the world of intercultural communication. Yet, interchange is an elusive pattern; it is not easy to identify or describe. Its chief virtues are the informality of its structure and its highly fluid operation. Under these circumstances, we shall save a bit of time by saying what interchange is not.

Interchange, first of all, is not very much like the authority dyad. In many respects, an interchange dyad is the opposite of an authority dyad. Where the authority dyad operates like an automobile with a single set of controls, the interchange dyad operates more like an airplane with dual controls. In the interchange dyad, both communicators decide the start/stop times, both communicators participate in the switch/share operations, and both execute the revise/elaborate routines as required. An interchange dyad operates under shared or mutual control.

An interchange dyad operates to achieve a *mutual* purpose. An authority dyad operates to achieve a purpose that is individually determined by the authority-communicator. Not so with the interchange dyad. The fact that the interchange dyad does operate to achieve a mutual purpose, however, requires some additional skills.

In the interchange dyad, the purpose determines the moment-by-moment structure. This is one reason that the structure that does exist often escapes both a participant and an observer. Another reason is that interchange, when it works smoothly, very intensively involves the participants in communication. Two hours of interchange can be very tiring. There is very little rest time for either participant in an interchange dyad. When interchange works well, both communicators may become completely unaware of clock time.

Interchange dyads operate intraculturally within a community when conditions are favorable. In fact, tutorials and interviews that turn out well from the view of the participants have the possibility of shifting into an interchange structure. When the tutor remarks, "I think I learned more than the tutee did today," it is quite clear the tutorial has moved toward an interchange structure. Equally, when an interviewer reports, "I got so interested in what we were talking about, that I forgot to write down the answers," the interview has moved toward an interchange.

In the observation and practice of intercultural communication, the authority structure and the interchange structure *overlap* somewhat. During the course of communication, when "things do not go well," there is usually a movement toward the authority structure and, hence, to tutorial or an interview.

Because of its central importance to intercultural communication, we shall continue the discussion of intercultural interchange throughout the book. For most communicators, interchange is easier *intra*culturally than *inter*culturally. Yet, in spite of an occasional monstrous problem, the possibilities for the particular dyad and for intercultural communication, in general, are so great that we must engage in intercultural interchange.

AUDIO AND VISUAL

Intercultural communication is an area of study and practice within the much larger field of human communication. By custom, certain topics have become of central interest and others have not. For instance, print in the form of literature is not generally considered an essential part of intercultural communication. Similarly, in an early chapter, the large group in the telecomnet—radio and TV—was identified as part of cross-cultural but not of intercultural communication.

Intercultural communication is centered in interaction. The communicators have an opportunity to change each other in fundamental ways. Our concept of intercultural interchange fits squarely into this two-way interactive context.

Intercultural communication occurs in dyadic and small group systems operating in either a transcomnet or telecomnet. The transcomnet system, in which one communicator travels to the "place" where the other resides or, alternately, they meet at some agreed on "place," involves both audio and visual aspects of communication. The telecomnet system, at the moment, involves only the audio. Somewhat later, the picture–phone will provide a two-way audiovisual capacity.

Almost any communication system operates more reliably when both the audio and visual capacities are used. When two communicators from the same cultural background say and repeat words, the task is performed about 15 percent more accurately when they can both see and hear each other. In general, the same finding holds for saying and repeating sentences and entire messages. Communication is more reliable when it is both audio and visual, when communicators can both see and hear each other.

There are a number of simple examples of a dyad or small group operating satisfactorily with only the audio or the visual. A deaf person may learn to lip-read. A blind person learns to "see" the braille print with his fingers. Silent movies had their day, and an occasional comic still practices the ancient art of mime. Most frequent, of course, is the audio-only telephone. The absence of either the audio or visual capacity requires certain adjustments, but it does not prohibit communication.

On the other hand, there sometimes arises in intercultural communication a situation in which the audio and visual seem to convey different and conflicting information. These conflicting informational patterns are usually discussed under the title of verbal and nonverbal communication (Mehrabian, 1972; Hinde, 1972; Birdwhistell, 1970).

Sometimes perplexing things happen. A certain head movement or hand movement means yes or good in one culture and no or bad in another. There is a troublesome mismatch between what is heard and what is seen. Those who have become most interested in such matters have separated them into verbal and nonverbal categories. We shall unseparate or recombine them and treat them as part of the more general audiovisual problems that sometimes arise at the intercommunity, international, and world levels.

INFORMATION

The cultural patterns of any community can be observed. Some of the patterns in a community will be treated as problems by the members of the community. Other patterns will be treated as possibilities. While it is interesting for the traveler to note that the patterns which are treated as problems in one community are treated as possibilities in another, the present point is only obliquely related to the shifting nature of problems/possibilities. The immediate concern is that both problems and possibilities will move some of the members of a community to seek information from outside the community. The simple quest for information is the major force behind intercultural communication.

Most of the information in the world is stored in the brains of the members of the many communities of the world. No one man and no single community store in their brains all of the world's information, though there was a brief time when some United States citizens living abroad seemed not to have discovered that fact. Through the daily living in a community within a particular set of cultural patterns, information is acquired and stored. In the sense Dubos suggested, each man's store of information is unique. Each community's store of shared information is also unique. Each culture makes some things obvious and obscures others.

For the solution of identified problems, quite often a rather simple exchange of information is all that is required. A problem that exists in one community has been solved by another community. Communication between the members of the two communities may be all that is required.

For the development of new possibilities, a quite different set of circumstances arises. Often, a possibility is only vaguely suspected. Most of the persons within a community do not sense the possibility or the opportunity it presents. A community member engages in intercultural interchange with a member from another community with a similar sense of the possible. Together, they shape their purpose for communicating, and together they talk the matter through to its conclusion. To be sure, they call up and use information from their stores, and they mutually benefit from the fact that they possess quite different information. But if their intercultural interchange goes well, they will, in the process of combining their joint store of information, begin to create new information. The names applied to the processes of information invention and creation are synergy and serendipity, and a later unit is devoted to the special power that these twin processes bring to intercultural communication.

Information is usually defined as "that which reduces uncertainty." By contrast, living out life within the cultural web of a particular community, most especially at a time of rapid change, generates uncertainty. As that uncertainty becomes identified, it is usually described as either a problem or as a possibility. In a philosophical sense, the total range of the problems and the possibilities of mankind, present and future, exists within the cultural framework of a community. To an extent, what is defined as a problem and what is defined as a possibility are a matter of choice. The traveler is often struck by two communities, otherwise quite similar, which differ in the proportion of communication time they spend talking over their problems and the time they spend talking-into-being some of their possibilities. The difference is the difference between stagnation and development.

Information as a resource has a unique characteristic. Take a particular item of money. If you give a coin to a stranger, he has one coin more than before and you have one less. So it is with most material resources. But information operates differently. If you "give" information to a stranger, both you and he have that same information. His gain is not your loss. If you and he exchange information, both of you gain. But beyond that, if you and he, in the process of exchanging information, invent new information, then the exchanging of information "pays off," somewhat as compound interest pays off in a savings account in which the loan machinery and the saver's cash make money for both parties (Bagdikian, 1971; *Information Technology*, 1972; Schroder, Driver, and Streufert, 1967).

But the delicate balance in a communication system requires a particular communicative association. We turn next to the notion of a communicative association that facilitates the inventive and creative exchange of information.

COMMUNICATIVE ASSOCIATION

The intercultural dyad, which is the focus of our attention, is organized for some mutual purpose by two communicators. Each one of these two communicators is "unique and unprecedented." Each one, up to the moment he begins communicating, has developed as a result of the interaction of his own individual self with the cultural forces of the home community and, perhaps, the world community. Each Japanese is easily distinguishable from every other Japanese. Japanese are easily distinguished from Norwegians in appearance, to be sure, but as much by the consequences of culture. In an intercultural dyad, then, both communicators stand as separate human beings. Their intercultural dyad is doubly "unique and unprecedented."

The observation is made with some frequency today that all men are brothers. But as every person who grows up in a large family knows, all brothers are different. For the problems and possibilities of interest in intercultural communication, it is both fortunate and necessary that these differences exist (Kleinjans in Richstad and Harms, 1973).

Quite often, the first experience a person has in attempting to communicate with a stranger from a distant community is a perplexing one. He is likely to think the stranger "talks funny." The stranger is different. And for many members of many communities, the stranger who is "different" is also inferior. It is a substantial step from the "different and inferior" evaluation to a tight-lipped tolerance. "He's different, all right, but who am I to say if that's good or bad?" A further step takes the community member on to a realization that the cultures of the many communities of man are equally valid ways in which men live out their lives. Intercultural interchange requires an additional step. President John F. Kennedy urged us "to make the world free for diversity." What slowly emerges is the appreciation that the solutions of problems and the development of possibilities depend directly on the existence of a wide range of alternatives embodied in the many communities. A bit further along, one begins to wonder if it will be necessary to build cultural sanctuaries where cultures which are endangered by increased intercultural communication might be enabled to flourish. It is a long road from the "different and inferior" to "enable the difference to flourish." That road is not yet well traveled.

In considering the communicative association that can be built by two persons in a dyad, many of the great concerns of moral philosophy and religion are touched upon. It is worth pointing out at this juncture that the Christian guide to behavior, the golden rule, is inadequate in intercultural communication. In monetary matters, the world is no longer on the gold standard. Similarly, in this communicating world, there exists no single rule which is an adequate guide for behavior in all situations. Nor, I might add, is a new rule likely to be developed in six easy lessons. Fortunately, intercultural communication is a richer endeavor than that.

At this point, communicative association as a concept requires closer examination. In the dictionary sense of the term, an association is formed for a mutual purpose. The term purpose usually implies a pooling of resources with the expectation of producing something of value out of those pooled resources.

The concept of communicative association involves additional purpose, however. Some definitions of communication view the first task of human communication as that of improving human relationships. Additionally some students of intercultural communication extend that same goal into the field of intercultural communication. Herein lie some potential and unnecessary difficulties.

From the view of communicative association, the matter appears in this way. Not all associations are primarily communicative ones; only some are. Not all human relationships are concerned with purposeful communication; only some are. That range of purposeful and communicative relationships, a working range, is called communicative association.

The structural patterns discussed earlier, the authority dyad and the interchange dyad, are interwoven with the concept of communicative association. The structure of a communication system also appears at another level, as a type of association between the communicators. In the authority dyad, the association is quite formal and may be precisely described. In the interchange dyad, the reverse is observed. The association is informal and fluid.

The crucial matter, however, is the relationship between association and purpose. In the authority dyad, the authority-communicator preselects the purpose and regulates the association between himself and the other communicator, toward the end of achieving his purpose. In the interchange dyad, the two communicators specify their *mutual* purpose, and they associate in a way that permits them to achieve it. Their association is guided by the requirements of their mutual purpose.

More specifically, every mutual purpose requires the exchange of information for its achievement. Equally, the start/stop, switch/share, and revise/elaborate operations all depend on an appropriate and delicate balance in communicative association. It is this elegant interplay of information *and* association that most exactly characterizes intercultural interchange. To achieve that elegant interplay, problems of communication must be solved as they arise, and when they are, the possibilities are enormous. The synergy swings and the serendipity sparkles.

SYNERGY AND SERENDIPITY

The terms synergy and serendipity have been carefully planted in a few of the earlier paragraphs. If the terms are a regular part of your vocabulary, you may well have wondered for a moment why a technical term from system theory and a word from the title of a flippant story were placed side by side. Let me show their role in intercultural communication.

Some of the peculiar characteristics of information were mentioned a bit earlier. In particular, in an intercultural dyad in which two communicators exchange information, they quite often, as they are communicating, *invent new information.* Technically, that invented information results from the working of synergy. Oversimply, synergy is what happens when you add one and one and really get three or a little more. The observation that information, unlike most other resources, can be shared but not given away is an instance of serendipity. It is not the type of discovery that can be achieved by a direct application of logic. Thus, serendipity is more than a little like love!

Besides all that, synergy and serendipity are fun concepts. They let us add a little levity and humor to the sometimes needlessly sober undertaking of intercultural communication.

Synergy

Synergy is a process that may operate in an organized system with a favorable structure. In the case of communication, in an authority structure in which messages are prepared and transmitted, there is little or no opportunity for synergy to operate. The interchange structure, however, is favorable to the process of synergy.

In an intercultural dyad operating in an interchange structure, high synergy may be expected. Two culturally dissimilar communicators have equivalent stores of information. As they attempt to achieve a mutual purpose, they create or develop a unique message. When interchange is working well, such a message contains elements of information contributed by both communicators. In addition, it will contain elements that are a direct result of the process of combining information from two culturally different stores. Thus, in the details of a message itself can be found instances of synergy.

It follows that the purpose, the *mutual* purpose, of an intercultural dyad may also be a purpose that could not be achieved in an *intra*cultural dyad. Many of the intercultural and intracultural purposes will be similar. But some purposes, particularly some of those relating to interpersonal relationships, can best be and at times can only be achieved in an intracultural dyad. Equally, some purposes can only be achieved in an intercultural dyad in which the process of synergy is at work (Benedict, 1970; Maslow and Honigmann, 1970).

Serendipity

Serendipity is the happy art and fortunate science of looking for one thing and finding something else which is better. Like synergy, it requires a favorable structure in a communication system. Serendipity does not often occur in an authority dyad. The interchange dyad, especially the intercultural interchange dyad, provides a favorable set of conditions for serendipity to break through (Dale, 1971).

A particular instance of serendipity is not predictable. But its growing grounds are quite well known and resemble those for humor. Ecological mutation provides a convenient analogy. A very small percentage of the organisms in a species are different from the others in one or more noticeable and significant ways. Most such mutations are not successful, and the mutated organism is eliminated. But once in a while a mutated organism survives and may, in time, prevail. Much the same process is at work in the gradual changes that continue to occur in human communication (Remer, 1965).

Most research hypotheses—the new questions that guide research—have a strong serendipitous quality to them. These hypotheses are not entirely predictable from previous knowledge. They spring up. A recent example in communication studies came out of a rerecognition that the global transportation network is also a communication network. Thus, with two networks to contend with, the question arises, "When can one of these networks be *substituted* for the other?" Then a set of related questions arises on whether it is possible to communicate rather than commute to work, thereby relieving the traffic problem, and to what extent face-to-face association is necessary for long-term human communication, and so forth. One little serendipity can go a long way.

In the moment-to-moment unfolding of intercultural communication, there are many little mismatches. Most of these mismatches require a bit of revision, and that is all. But every mismatch of a word, a sentence, or a larger informational element contains the possibility of a serendipity. In other words, the experienced intercultural communicator is alert to the possibilities inherent in those unexpected things that quite naturally occur in intercultural communication. Serendipity is the reward for a certain lighthearted vigilance.

Humor itself often springs forth from the same stuff as serendipity. What is probably the oldest traveler's story in the world illustrates the point.

Tourist A: How do you say the name of this place? Is it Ha*w*aii or Ha*v*aii?

Tourist B: I don't know. Let's ask someone who knows.

Tourist A: Sir, how do you pronounce the name of this place?

Someone who knows: Havaii.

Tourist B: Thank you, sir.

Someone who knows: You're *v*elcome.

In this small story, there is both a touch of humor and a dash of serendipity.

THE HUMAN RIGHT TO COMMUNICATE

In this chapter on intercultural interchange, several concepts have been introduced. Taken together, they add up to a new human right: *The Right of Man to Communicate.*

We are indebted to Jean d'Arcy, formerly with the United Nations and now of Paris, for advancing this notion. D'Arcy suggests that the time has come to review and revise Article 19 of the *Universal Declaration of Human Rights.* Article 19 contains a key phrase: "to seek, receive and impart information." In essence, Article 19 is concerned with freedom of information (d'Arcy, 1969).

Article 20 is also of concern for intercultural communication. The question of human association is dealt with in Article 20. It specifies that a human must be free to join an association as he chooses, and he must be free not to join an association. He may choose to join; he may choose not to join. I see Article 20 as having direct bearing on the matter of communicative association.

A concept of the Right of Man to Communicate combines the basic notions of Article 19 and Article 20 and extends them.

Those of us concerned with intercultural communication have a special interest in this proposed Right to Communicate. If we refer back to the two world communication networks, the transcomnet and the telecomnet, it is easy to see why we have this special interest. The networks make it *possible* for any man to communicate with any other man for some mutual purpose. If any man does not enjoy the right to communicate, in a direct sense, all other humans are also deprived of their right to communicate. If it is to become a meaningful right, the Right to Communicate must become a *mutual* right—for all of us.

Intercultural interchange includes both the exchange of information and communication association. As discussed here, communicative association requires two-way communication facilities. Both serendipity and synergy depend on a two-way interchange structure. And, intercultural interchange is communication for a mutual purpose.

There is an additional point about association embodied in Article 20. A human cannot be required to join an association. This suggests that in addition to the Right to Communicate, any human also has the Right *not* to Communicate. From this point, it follows that there will be a natural and self-imposed constraint on the amount of communication a person chooses to engage in. Obviously, as worldwide intercultural communication becomes more routinely possible, the problem of communication overload becomes more probable. Therefore, a self-determined *privacy* becomes a necessary filter that the individual imposes between himself and the rest of the world.

IN ADDITION

In an area as diversified as intercultural communication, it is necessary to develop a habit of looking through many potentially useful resource materials quickly. Those that appear most useful to you can be selected for more careful study. For example, examine Jaffe and Feldstein, *Rhythms of Dialogue*; Matson and Montagu, *The Human Dialogue*; Pope and Siegman, *Studies in Dyadic Communication*; Birdwhistell, *Kinesics and Context*; Hinde, *Non-Verbal Communication*; Moyers, *Listening to America*; Bagdikian, *The Information Machines*; and Remer, *Serendipity and the Three Princes.* Also, look through McHale, *World Facts and Trends.*

The concept of synergy is of particular importance. Read the articles on Ruth Benedict's notions of synergy, edited by Maslow and Honigmann, as well as that written by Harris. There is also an interesting article on serendipity by Dale.

These first three chapters provide a foundation for the study of intercultural communication. It must be stressed that this is only *one* of several possible foundations. It is *a* way; it is not *the* way. Other quite different approaches are included in the bibliographic materials. See, for instance, Oliver, *Communication and Culture in Ancient India and China*; Triandis, *The Analysis of Subjective Culture*; Prosser, *Intercommunication Among Nations and Peoples*; Rogers and Shoemaker, *Communication of Innovations*; and Lerner and Schramm, *Communication and Change in Developing Countries.* In particular, examine the article on cross-cultural communication by Gardner.

The concept of the Right to Communicate pulls together and focuses the content of the first three chapters. Two articles by Jean d'Arcy on this topic are very important. See his article in the *EBU Review* and also his article in the book on the *International Law of Communication*, edited by Edward McWhinney. Study the wording of Articles 19, 20, and 27 of the *Universal Declaration of Human Rights* (pp. 127–132). We do not yet have a set of principles of a declaration of the right of man to communicate (see p. 136). Under what conditions might it be possible to evolve a *Declaration of Communication Rights for Mankind*?

Read the introductory material for the Projects (pp. 137–140) and complete Project I (pp. 141–143).

4

Intercommunity Communication

The preceding three chapters provided a foundation for the study of intercultural communication. A worldview is made possible and necessary by the transcomnet and the telecomnet. The interrelationship between culture and communication was explored. And in the previous chapter, an examination was made of the special possibilities inherent in intercultural interchange.

In this chapter, the first stage of communication development beyond the home community is taken as the topic. Most of us first encounter this when we "go away" to school, by being bused to kindergarten, traveling "across town" to high school, or "going off" to college in another state, or when we "go off" to work. The problems in such intercommunity communication are usually immediately apparent; the possibilities are often less visible.

In the next chapter, the second stage of development beyond the home community—international communication—is the topic of interest.

INTRODUCTION

For this chapter, we shall adopt the point of view of an observer with experience in international communication and with wide experience in a variety of intercommunity communication settings. Such an observer retains sympathy for the large problems at the intercommunity level, while at the same time he is aware that even larger possibilities also are involved.

A further point needs to be stressed. In an area such as intercultural communication, wide agreement exists only on quite limited matters. I neither expect nor wish that you memorize each page and recite it thereafter as the ultimate truth. What I do hope is that you will read an entire chapter and discuss it with others before arriving at a "tentative" conclusion. Further, the projects at the end of the book will help you clarify your key questions.

In that the study of intercultural communication on the scale attempted here is quite new, it is hoped that the reader who finds himself in substantial *dis*agreement with a chapter or unit of a chapter will undertake to draft a complete alternative. Intercultural interchange within a dyad depends on profiting from cultural diversity. There is no reason, of course, that intercultural interchange cannot be carried into the book area. I encourage and welcome alternative statements—as I hope you do.

As we introduce the study of intercommunity communication, we must choose the terms for our discussion carefully. There are many "loaded" words, such as correct pronunciation, standard English, sloppy speech, and substandard dialect, that interfere with a serious discussion of the problems and possibilities. In our role of observer from another developmental stage, we shall attempt to use terms which are more nearly neutral, though, I must admit, not quite as much fun.

To begin with, let us introduce the concept of *specialization.* When a person does one thing very well, when he spends thousands of hours perfecting his skill in that particular thing, he is unable to develop skill in doing other things that also require large quantities of time to master. To take an obvious example, an open-heart surgeon has general skill in the practice of medicine, but he chooses to specialize in the repair and replacement of the human heart. If he chooses to specialize in the heart, he will not also specialize in brain surgery, or ulcer repair, or a dozen other specialties one could name. Within a university, a student may major in—become a specialist in—one, or at most, two or three fields. It is highly likely that any particular student might do very well in a half dozen different fields, but it is equally likely that he will be unable to specialize in as many as six fields. Specialization of any kind trades depth for breadth. Hence, we say that a specialist is narrow. He does one thing well, and that seems to be all he does.

In the case of communication within a community, the outside observer detects the same process of specialization at work (Williams, 1970). A child learns, to the fine details, to communicate as the other members of his community do. Initially his family, and particularly his mother, will be most influential in developing his specialization. The extreme cases are instructive here. In the event the mother stutters badly, the child may learn to speak stutteringly. Equally, in a family where both parents have cleft palates, their child will likely learn to speak with the nasal quality that characterizes the cleft-palate speech. A normal hearing child born to deaf parents may learn a nonverbal sign language instead of the more usual verbal speech patterns.

The child learns to communicate with the members of his family first, and slightly later, with other members of his community. Given the very large number of communication patterns that exist within the various communities of the world, his accomplishments merit the term specialization. First and foremost, *the child becomes a communication specialist within his home community.*

If the schools the child attends have teachers from his home community, the "way he talks"—his specialty—will be regarded as "normal." If he also goes to the higher grades in his community with teachers from his home community, he is likely to graduate from high school without being much more concerned about the way he communicates than he is about the way he breathes. But if he continues into a community college in that same community, he is likely, then, if not before, to have to communicate with teachers drawn from communities far from his own.

The discovery of intercommunity problems in communication may come early, as it does for the young children who are "bused" to other communities to attend school. It may come late, as it does for the young adult who enjoys the advantage of growing up in a stable but somewhat isolated community. But whenever the problem develops, it is likely to be treated not as the natural and expected result of a particular specialization, but as something which is different and by definition inferior to some other "good" way of communicating. Any way that last statement is said, it is received as bad news by the person who is judged to have "the problem."

The area of intercommunity communication, as much as any problem/possibility area I know, desperately needs the detached analysis of the observer as cautious optimist. To tell a person he talks "bad" is akin to telling him that he was born into a hopelessly messy package. Very few of us escape being penalized for our childhood specialization. Hours of often humiliating and embarrassing, though well-intended, instruction are part of the penalty we pay. To survive all this, a sense of humor is needed but is often absent.

THE PROBLEM/POSSIBILITY AREA

The following discussion of problems and possibilities assumes the communicators under discussion pass as normal within their respective home communities. Another way of getting at the same point would be with the following question:

> Is there at least one person—a family member or friend—with whom you communicate successfully?

Most communicators will reply *yes* and add that there is more than one, there are indeed several persons or quite a number of them, but never that there are thousands and thousands. However, from time to time, a person will reply to such a question that no one, not even his mother, is fit to talk with; everyone he knows is too ignorant to communicate with, no one can be trusted, and besides, the world will end tomorrow. A person who replies in such a fashion is assumed to have enough *intra*community problems in communication to keep him busy for a while and is, therefore, placed outside of the present discussion. At any rate, such persons constitute a small percentage of most home communities.

The study of intercultural communication deals with the advantages inherent in cultural diversity and human variety. The term *cultural diversity*, in the course of this book, will refer to the cultural differences (and similarities) among the members of a community considered as a group or collectivity. The term *human variety* will refer to the individual differences (and similarities) within a community. Thus, by definition, cultural diversity will refer to differences among communities, and human variety will refer to differences within a community. There are differences (and similarities) between and within communities.

The distinction between diversity and variety becomes important in every intercultural dyad. The two communicators come from culturally different communities. Equally important, they are individuals. Cultural information about the community is useful; specific information about the individual communicator is essential. Both diversity and variety figure in the communication patterns in the intercultural dyad.

A word of caution is in order. In most communities, there exists a small group of persons, including a few professional communication scholars, who become specialists in creating the insoluble and paradoxical problems of communication. They get hung up on the fact that human communication is at best imperfect. They look for examples of communication failure and are overwhelmed by how many "barriers" they discover. These folks seem never to detect the *possibilities* which are an equally legitimate part of intercultural communication. I call them the eager pessimists.

The Problem Area

Any community that has well-defined boundaries, intensive interaction among community members within those boundaries, and comparatively little purposeful communication with others from outside the community creates the conditions that develop communication specialists. Exactly the same conditions make the likelihood of problems in intercommunity communication quite high. All that is required is a change in some area that brings members of two or more communities into contact with one another. A change in school enrollment procedures, busing for example, or opening a large factory that hires persons from several communities will suffice. The change that creates the need for frequent and purposeful intercommunity communication is, of itself, of little consequence once the forces are set in motion.

"The problem" is typically stated by some organized group—school, management, and so forth—in terms so broad that it is difficult to determine what, if anything, could be done to reduce that problem. At one time or another, such intercommunity problems have been ascribed to bad breeding, genetic inferiority, lack of culture, poverty, and the wrong religion. A complete list would be very, very long. There is one point of consistency. Steadfastly, the group that discovers the problem defines that problem as residing in some other identifiable group.

The first step for anyone undertaking the thankless task of reducing the problem to a tolerable level—given community specialization processes, the problem cannot be eliminated—is to word the problem in a way that makes it clear what needs to be done. Such a move is quite unpopular with those who discover the problem, those who are said to have the problem, and, often, with those professionals at work trying to solve the problem.

An observer who has watched a problem go full cycle in other intercommunity settings has a number of hard questions to ask, and he requires answers that relate to those specific questions

(Mager and Pipe, 1970). The first question is: Is the problem important, or will it go away when the moon changes or another interesting problem comes along to replace it? If the problem is of the magnitude that creates difficulty in intercommunity intercultural communication, then the question: Is it a skill or attitude problem, or some combination of the two?

In some cases, a genuine problem in communication skill is involved. In a broad sense, the level of communication skill in any one community *for its purposes* is probably about equal to the communication skill in any other community for its purposes. But, the purposes of intercommunity intercultural communication will more closely resemble the *intra*cultural communication purposes within some communities than it does within others. Thereby, an advantage falls to members of those communities whose intracommunity purposes resemble most closely the *inter*community purposes.

More importantly, there is a wide variety of communication skill represented in any community. Some of the communicators from every community may be expected to encounter moderate to severe communication difficulties outside the community.

The communicator who is singled out for communication training usually has the question, "Why me?" The answer to that question is, "It will save you headaches, save you time if you do." But he may persist, "I talk well with my family and friends, yet I am required to have additional training." The answer often lies in the technical requirement of a job or an anticipated job.

For instance, assume two young ladies of equal communication skill obtain jobs at about the same salary. One works as a seamstress in the back room of a dress shop and takes her orders from an older lady who is a longtime friend of her mother's. Her communication skills are almost certainly adequate. The other works for a telephone company as a switchboard operator. Her skills in intercommunity communication might not be adequate. She might expect to have to type 60 words per minute for a job that specified such typing speed. But the requirement of 90 percent mutual intelligibility with a specified variety of other communicators does not make the same kind of sense to her or to most of us, even though 60 words per minute and 90 percent intelligibility are similar job requirements.

Where the problem can be identified specifically, such as low word intelligibility, there are a number of ways of reducing the problem. Formal training is one way, supervised on-the-job practice is another, and carefully arranged feedback is a third (Black and Singh in Malmberg, 1968:105).

At times, basic information processing skills are adequate in a given situation, but still a problem exists. The problem lies not in the intelligibility area related to information processing but in the acceptability area related to communicative association (Quirk and Svartvik, 1966).

When attitude rather than skill is at the heart of a problem, a number of questions require asking. Is communication punishing to the communicator? If so, remove the punishment. Is noncommunication rewarding the communicator? In that case, arrange positive consequences for communicating. Is communication important? If not, arrange for communication to have desirable consequences. Finally, if there are obstacles, remove those obstacles.

Quite often, in intercommunity intercultural communication, say in a dyadic system, the problems of skill and attitude interweave with information processing and communicative association. For instance, if Communicator A asks B to revise a word or statement, and B *ignores* the request, there are a number of factors operating that make communication difficult and may interrupt it.

In intercommunity communication, it is important to discover whether the problem is basically one of skill or attitude or some combination of the two. Secondly, it is important to determine if the problem has most bearing on information processing or communicative association. Once the problem is clearly analyzed, the way to reducing it need not be—but sometimes is—far away.

The Possibility Area

The possibilities of intercommunity communication are seldom immediately obvious. First of all, when intercommunity communication is undertaken, the "spur of necessity" is often involved. At times, it is only one individual who "goes into" a new community. At other times, a substantial percentage of the members of a community may come into fresh contact with a substantial number of the members from some other social group, or a new community may be organized by members from numerous different communities.

The possibilities that may arise from intercommunity communication should be considered on three levels: the economic; the educational; and the social.

The economic aspects of intercommunity communication are widely studied. To begin with, most lines of work have particular vocabularies, jargons, and styles of communicating associated with them. Thus, one part of every specialty is a specialized and technical way of communicating. The individual who masters a new technical jargon as quickly as he masters the other aspects of a new job can expect to advance on schedule. But the new employee who does not master the specialized style of communication required on the job can expect to be held back or passed up for promotion. Thus, the economic consequences for the individual can be substantial (Williams, 1970:1).

The educational possibilities are entwined with school requirements. Schools in many communities and nations view part of their task as preparing the student to operate "upstairs" in the large-scale establishment culture. The individual communicator who makes the developmental step from his own community-based style of communication to the more general or "standard" model of the school participates more fully in the full range of school activities. He does not have to take remedial courses, he can participate fully in classroom discussion, and he is not regarded as "funny" by his schoolmates (Cazden in Griffith and Miner, 1972:307).

The individual communicator, then, who masters "school talk" has the possibilities offered by formal education fully available. If he does not master it, of course, he lives out his school days as a stranger in a strange land—a likely early dropout.

The third class of possibilities that arise from intercommunity communication is a greater variety of friends, more diversity in interpersonal relationships, etc. These possibilities are not usually pursued directly. A person does not usually go out and apply for a new friend as he would apply for a new job, nor does he enroll in a "class in friends" as he might enroll in a class in algebra. So, wider social contacts and a richer diversity in friendships are major possibilities that arise for the communicator who reaches out beyond the limits of his community to engage in intercommunity communication. But such associations are usually a serendipitous by-product of task-oriented on-the-job or in-the-school communication that first succeeds for the individual in one or more other important respects.

We turn next to three case studies of intercommunity intercultural communication.

PYGMALION IN ENGLAND

The Pygmalion love story comes to us from Greek mythology. Pygmalion carves from stone a beautiful woman, more beautiful than any living woman, and as he sculpts he falls in love with the statue. The goddess Aphrodite brings the statue to life. Pygmalion names his sculpted lady Galatea, marries her, and lives in perfect happiness ever after (Moncrieff, 1934:121).

George Bernard Shaw based a play on the Pygmalion myth (Shaw, 1948). The play—entitled *Pygmalion*—also has its Pygmalion and Galatea. Pygmalion is embodied as a professor of phonetics; phonetics is a worldwide science of pronunciation. Galatea is a Cockney-speaking girl named Eliza Doolittle, who sells flowers for a living. In the course of the play, Professor Higgins transforms Eliza from a Cockney speaker to a speaker of "Received Pronunciation"—she learns to speak like a real lady. The Shaw stage play of *Pygmalion* was later adapted for the Broadway musical, *My Fair Lady*, and then for a movie by the same name.

In the preface that Shaw wrote to *Pygmalion*, he points out that many persons are forever cut off from "high employment" because of their particular way of speaking.

> . . . for the encouragement of people troubled with accents that cut them off from all high employment, I may add that the change wrought by Professor Higgins in the flower girl is neither impossible nor uncommon. . . . But the thing has to be done scientifically, or the last stage of the aspirant may be worse than the first.

However, in the play itself, the key test that Eliza must pass is not an on-the-job demonstration of skill, but rather that she pass as a lady at a social affair attended by "high-class" residents of London.

Eliza does pass this "social acceptability" test, attracts the attention of an eligible, high-class, young bachelor named Freddy Eynsford Hill, and, as Shaw notes in the postscript to the play, eventually marries him. Freddy and Eliza eventually open a small flower shop in a railway station. So much for Pygmalion and his Galatea.

The Shaw play *Pygmalion* embodies many of the aspirations of those involved in intercommunity communication:

training in communication
seeking of high employment
social acceptability
social mobility

In communities where social class is unrecognized or unacknowledged, the situation may be difficult to analyze. Confusion exists even in the Shaw treatment.

In the preface, Shaw makes detailed reference to the relationship between dialect, or variety of English, or style of communication and the possibility of "high employment"—in short, professional employment. He asserts that the "science of phonetics" will enable a young person to mend his speech and thereby augment his fortune; in other words, he suggests that a young man will be more successful if he learns to talk like the lawyers, bankers, and "phoneticians" in his community. Indeed, phonetics can do just that, as many of us know.

Within the play itself, the test that Shaw, as playwright, proposes is that Eliza pass undetected for an evening, while engaging in social conversation with "high-class" Londoners.

I labor the point here a bit because often it is discussed under other guises. The *goal* is to enable the "learner" to gain employment of a particular type. The *test* is whether the "learner" communicates in a nonemployment social situation, quite often a classroom.

One can only speculate as to why Shaw did not have Eliza apply for a beginning managerial post in a bank, pass the employment interview, participate successfully in a bank-sponsored training program, and then utilize these skills on the job successfully.

The element of social class *change* is also submerged. Within any community there are a variety of subgroups. Some of these subgroups are formed on the joint basis of economic and educational factors. When groups are so formed, they merit the technical description of social class. Social class groupings, as do all other subgroupings within communities, result in an increase in within-group communication and a decrease in between-group communication.

The patterns of communication associated with different social groups within a community are readily recognized by nearly all community members (Harms, "Listener Comprehension," 1961). Community members are able to match a "voice" to a type of work or level of education. The two factors of job type and level of education describe quite accurately the many other features of social class. If you know how much schooling a man has and what he does for a living, you usually know whether he is of a high, middle, or low class.

The young person who engages in intercommunity communication quite often also engages in a change in social class. The upward mobility witnessed in America is often of this type.

Upward mobility, as in the case of Eliza, is quite often accomplished on an individual basis. The single person enters a new group. One part of the entry price almost always is that the newcomer conform to the established patterns of communication.

In England, the problem has been dealt with formally in the schools by teaching the style of communication known as RP or *Received Pronunciation.* For RP, the sounds of English are to be spoken in a prescribed way. Thus, variation from the prescribed RP pattern is assumed to identify a person as a member of a different and lower class. It is, of course, possible for almost anyone who chooses to do so to learn RP, if the conditions are appropriate. Many persons, including a majority of the world's English-speaking actors, have learned RP.

In intercommunity communication, there arise a few questions that are somewhat easier to ask than they are to answer. The first has to do with economic requirements and the other with social requirements.

Holding most "high-class" jobs requires particular communication skills, especially information-processing skills. In particular, information processing must be highly reliable or intelligible. Information processing at a satisfactory level of intelligibility is a first requirement, say, of a stockbroker, who "talks numbers for a living." Mistakes and misunderstandings are costly. Most training programs aim to make the "learner" intelligible to the persons with whom he will be communicating. But within such training programs, the matter of social acceptability often gets involved, in part because "the job" usually involves a certain amount of social life.

The interplay between information and association may or may not be of consequence, depending on certain assumptions. Shaw, for instance, felt that Eliza could no longer communicate successfully among her Cockney friends after she had learned RP. Eliza could not go home again. But others would argue that she had only learned to speak another variety of English and that she could shift back and forth as the situation warranted.

It should impress the observer that suggesting changes in styles of communicating, even small ones, often obtain strong reactions from the one who is to change. For instance, suppose you suggest to a friend that he mispronounces a particular word. It matters little what the word is or who the friend is. The reaction is quite predictable after the third or fourth such suggestion. Try it!

Within the life span of a single person and among the members of any family and any community, there will be a wide range of attitudes as to what happens to a person who learns to talk the way the folks in a nearby community talk. The attitude expressed will have much to do with economic advancement and social variety.

The work on specifying Received Pronunciation, RP, was done in London (Jones, 1962). It is a careful body of work, and on re-examination it yields additional information. Jones states that RP is the variety of English most often spoken by the educated persons in England *and that* RP is generally intelligible throughout the English speaking world. You can easily check the intelligibility of RP by tuning in to a newscast of the BBC World Service, as many persons around the world regularly do each day.

At exactly this point, we need to be very careful about the conclusions we draw. The BBC announcers are impressive in the similarity they exhibit in the details of pronunciation. They say the same words in the same way. And so long as we pay attention to a newscast monolog only, we are likely to remain most impressed with the *standardized* pronunciation we assume we hear. But there is another side to this matter of models.

Interestingly enough, another related but vastly different body of research has also been done in London (Bernstein in Williams, 1970:25). Bernstein distinguishes between what he calls restricted and elaborated codes. The two codes, or styles of communicating, differ in several respects. The restricted code is tied closely to a particular communication context; the elaborated code is not. The restricted code is particularistic (or specialized); the elaborated code is generalized. We shall add other details from the work of Bernstein as we go along.

The essential contrast between the work of Jones and Bernstein appears at first to be paradoxical. In his work, Jones seems to support the notion of a single standard of pronunciation, a particular way of saying a particular word. At first glance, this notion of a "received" standard seems also to resemble the restricted code. Bernstein, however, equates the elaborated code with a more general or universal style of communication. There are a number of mismatches of this kind which are not yet fully resolved.

The same semiparadoxical finding is reported for word intelligibility (Black and Singh In Malmberg, 1968:119). Black and Singh report that two kinds of words tend to be most intelligible: the short, familiar word with few sounds; and the long, less familiar word with many sounds. A word cannot be both short and long, both familiar and unfamiliar. I cite this example to illustrate that the questions in this area, at this time, are not yet simple, and the appropriate answers are not yet immediately obvious.

The term "Standard English" is a troublesome one. It suggests to many people that there is *a right form* and that any variation from that form is an error which is wrong. The standard is right; variation from that standard is wrong. This seems simple enough until one attempts to find standard speech "embodied" in the communication style of a real live communicator. When one does not simply assume that the standard exists, but attempts to find examples of it, the fun begins.

The BBC announcers are quite good examples of RP speakers. But move them out of the monolog and into a dialog and the situation changes. For in intercultural dialog, one does not observe dictionary-suggested consistency in pronunciation and other details of communication. What one observes is a great deal of revision and elaboration. We are again in a paradoxical situation in which the so-called Standard English communicators are those who are the most variable in practice. Standard English is better characterized by variability than by rigidity!

The story of Eliza Doolittle is a familiar and dramatic one. A review of the requirements of the well-made play would be helpful at this point but slightly beyond the scope of this book. As an alternative you may wish to set out in search of a person who acknowledges that he speaks a "flawless" Standard English of such quality that it should be used as a model for a World English. The questions are simple enough:

Do you speak Standard English?
Is the Standard English you speak flawless?
Would you be willing to have your flawless Standard English serve as a model for World English?

You may wish to record and analyze the answers you receive. The projects at the end of the book suggest ways of obtaining additional information.

BLACK AND WHITE IN AMERICA

Eliza Doolittle represents the occasional single individual who moves from a home community and studies, works, or resides for a time in another community. At this point, it matters very much what we view her purposes to be and how we talk about the strategies by which she achieves those purposes. In our discussion, we shall focus on the "public" aspects of informal social communication.

In the public domain, going by herself into a new community, she will learn one of the varieties of English, one of the styles of communication in that community. If she receives formal instruction, it will be in that standard or general style of communication, for example, RP or General American. If she learns from feedback on the job, it will be through interaction with fellow workers while she is working to achieve some general goal and a range of specific goals. Either way, the single "Eliza" will acquire the communication skills necessary to function, to perform in the "world establishment" or the world community. She will acquire World English, or more exactly, one of the World English*es*.

When a substantial number of the members of a community come in contact with the members of some other community at about the same time, the situation changes (Pinkney, 1969). And because most of the statements about these changes are multipurpose and emotionally loaded, we must examine the situation carefully as we proceed (Smith, Arthur L., 1972). First, let me restate that my concern here is with intercultural rather than cross-cultural communication. Most often the concern is with a single dyad, in that most intercultural communication occurs in dyadic systems, and most communicators engage in purposeful communication in but one dyad at a time. At times, intercommunity intercultural communication also occurs in small group systems organized by communicators from two or several communities. Recall that our viewpoint is that of the system observer who has substantial experience in international communication.

In every family, in every community, any measure of communication skill shows both similarities and differences in that skill. Let us emphasize the differences for a moment.

Twenty-five black children from a "culturally deprived" neighborhood in Detroit were tested on the Illinois Test of Psycholinguistic Ability (Sigel and Perry, 1968:122). The test results are varied. In the group of twenty-five, some children scored above, at, and below the norms for their age levels. More to the point, an even greater variability was found on the various subtests. Considering these twenty-five children to be members of a single "culturally deprived" group misses the essential point for intercultural communication. It is clearly shown that a wide range of skills exist within a group.

In the Hawaii Communication Test (HCT), a similar range of skill differences are shown to exist among the members of a single grade and at several grade levels (Byers, Coladarci, Harms, and Heinberg, 1971). Beyond that, individuals score differently on the various subtests, on sender-and-receiver roles, in same-sex versus alternate sex dyads, and so forth.

To speak of one group communicating with another group makes sense in cross-cultural communication, perhaps, but tends to obscure and confound the problems and/or possibilities in intercultural communication.

The "average man" stereotype is equally awkward. Given that variation in communication skill is a demonstrated fact, there is no convenient "model" available. What does suggest itself as an alternative is that some members of a subgroup (black) will be able to communicate successfully with certain members of another subgroup (white). It follows, then, that a particular black person and a particular white person may or may not be able to communicate successfully with each other for some purpose. It becomes a question of percentages.

More specifically, seven randomly selected black communicators paired with seven randomly selected white communicators, as measured by the HCT, can be expected to score on a wide range of possible scores. A few of the test dyads will score high. Some individual communicators will "tend to raise" the scores of the dyads in which they participate. Others will tend to lower them.

The point is that there is, among the members of any community-based microculture, a variety, a range of communication skills. This variety arises in part from presumed genetic endowment, age, place in the family, mobility, role in the community, and a larger set of other variables and factors.

The question is sometimes posed, "Should black children learn white dialect?" The question must be "unloaded" a bit before it can be dealt with (Baratz in Smith, Arthur L., 1972:3). Eliza Doolittle is again instructive. Should a black Eliza seek, or be required, to learn another variety of English, or should she learn several varieties of English? Or should she learn the strategies necessary for rapidly acquiring the style of any communication system in which she chooses to participate?

The questions of prescription and norms and standards are recurrent (Ray, 1963). Received Pronunciation, General American English, Standard Australian English, and Standard Canadian English, for instance, when spoken by announcers on the overseas radio news services of the various countries, are recognizably different varieties of English. Yet the news announcers are mutually intelligible. Specifically, a dyad composed of any two such speakers would likely score high on the HCT.

The problem of *communication* between and among blacks and whites in America, then, is, to a great extent, an artifact of definition. The more useful question is: how can those persons who wish to do so easily develop the skills necessary for communication in both their own home community microculture and the macroculture of the world community? The question has two sides.

Consider a particular dyad in which one of the two participants regularly communicates successfully with a wide variety of other world macroculture communicators. Can the more experienced participant use his additional experience to communicate successfully when the other has experience in only one or a limited number of closely related microcultures? More specifically, how can these two communicators adapt to each other to achieve their purpose? The answer to the question supposes that both B and W in this dyad will adapt to each other. In practice, this may be more difficult than first appears.

We need further to examine the literature in terms of the data that bear on the start/stop, switch/share, and revise/elaborate dimensions. The most crucial for the intercultural dyad appears to be the revise/elaborate. Bernstein's treatment of restricted and elaborated codes is particularly relevant (Bernstein in Williams, 1970:25).

The information-processing and communicative association factors also need to be examined. When information processing is accurate, or the revise/elaborate operations can make the matches necessary for accuracy in one or two reruns, information processing in a black–white, human–human dyad is likely to move smoothly. But if such is not the case, then the members of the dyad are likely to conclude they have a problem in communication. How they define the problem they think they have is of highest importance. At this point in time, the problem is likely to be defined—when skin colors are noticeably different—that the dark-skinned person causes the problem and requires "training" to remove those causes. If that definition stands, then, the stage is set for the "discussions at a distance" that characterized America in the late sixties.

Those of us who wish to come to terms with the problems of intercultural communication need to recognize that there are important things in the world other than human communication. Even though communication as a system is a subsystem of many other systems, it is not always the controlling system.

Though the *United States Constitution* declares all men are equal, in practice the United States has operated a *caste* system in some areas (Burling, 1970:117). As this particular situation undergoes change in social, economic, and educational areas, some of the problems we now identify as communication problems will be reduced to tolerable levels, and we will be able to concentrate on the possibilities—on the synergies and serendipities—that lie ahead.

PIDGIN IN HAWAII

Compared to most other places in the world, Hawaii is quite new. The first persons to settle Hawaii came by canoe from the south about a thousand years ago. In the ensuing years, the first immigrants settled on the major islands and increased in number to approximately 200,000 by 1778. At that time, the sailing ships of the Britisher Captain Cook rediscovered Hawaii. About half a century later, in 1820, the first missionaries sailed in from Boston. In the years that followed, new immigrants came from Korea, China, Japan, the Philippines, Australia, New Zealand, Samoa, the United States, and Canada, as well as from other areas of the world. The present population, excluding temporary visitors, numbers just over 800,000. The residents of Hawaii have an uncommon past (Carr, 1972).

The need for pidgin arose when immigrants came from around the Pacific during a relatively short span of a few decades. Apparently, the word pidgin is a variant of the Chinese word for business. And better than any other term, it captures the essence of the condition that propels the development of pidgins (Hall, 1962: 151). People with different natural languages, together, invent a new language to serve some limited and specific economic purpose (Nida and Fehderau, 1970:151).

Again, based on economic factors, the pidgin in Hawaii was English based. But it contains elements and patterns traceable to many languages and cultures (Carr, 1972).

Thus, pidgin represents an attempt on the part of communicators participating in a communication system to achieve communication for a mutual purpose. It follows that the more successful communicators are in achieving communication with one another, the more varieties of pidgin will be invented.

But then a curious thing begins to happen. As any particular communicator develops skill in communicating with persons from a number of different cultures, say 7 ± 2, what emerges as a dominant characteristic is his *adaptability*, his capacity to invent still other new varieties of pidgin. Thus, for a pidgin to retain the freshness of pidgin over time, those who speak pidgin must continue to reinvent it. To say the same thing another way, the conditions which led to development of the original pidgin must be recreated on a large scale at least once per generation.

When pidgin is learned from parents in the home, it ceases to be pidgin and becomes, technically speaking, a Creole (Carr, 1972: 34). Necessity gives way to convention. With little effort, one could argue that one should do away with "standard languages" and create the conditions in the world which would impel members of each microculture to develop their own unique and specialized style of communication and provide opportunities for some community members to develop skill in inventing instant and very short-term pidgins. In a special sense, each intercultural communication system that operates successfully can be seen to be in the process of inventing its own pidgin. But one has to be careful not to push the point further than the data allow.

In Hawaii, then, pidgins first arose to meet limited, face-to-face information requirements for economic purposes. A bit later, they became the style of communication in many homes as well. And in this subtle shift from information to association, a number of problems arose. The flexibility became frozen.

But the conditions in Hawaii changed. The single most powerful factor was the growth of world communication networks and, with those networks, the emergence of a World English which functions in many ways on a global basis, as pidgin does for the limited purposes in a small community. Pidgin is to the temporary microculture as World English is to the World Macroculture. In both cases, the most distinctive characteristic is adaptability to the immediate requirements of a particular communication system.

The changes which occurred in Hawaii are instructive. Today the island counties are part of a centralized state government. The state is part of the United States, and the United States, in turn, is one of the United Nations. Many of the early businesses in Hawaii—including those which first "imported labor" from Asia—are now multi-national companies; many of the businesses in Hawaii are branches of world business organizations. The verbal communication style of world business and world politics is World English.

When a pidgin becomes stabilized (frozen) into a Creole, it also appears to shift from an elaborating to a restricting code. This shift is important in situations in which the revise/elaborate operations are critical. One such place is in the job interview. In an intercultural dyad with a pidgin speaker, the interviewer, say for a multi-national company, does not receive adaptive answers to his questions. He is unable, for instance, to assess the technical qualifications of a young engineer and decides against hiring. Technical skill locked in a local English is restricted in its usefulness.

It is relatively easy for the pidgin speaker to acquire World English if the conditions are right. One set of "conditions" was developed and embodied in a multi-media, performance-centered training program developed at the University of Hawaii (Harms, 1969, 1972; Heinberg, Harms, and Yamada, 1970). However, it is equally easy to worry the pidgin speaker with the details of language in a way that results in his deciding that he is ignorant and unable to learn.

Again, it is important to point out that acquisition of World English does not result in loss of pidgin, any more than learning World French results in loss of World English, though often some of the spontaneity may seem to be lost.

In its origins, pidgin, like World English, arises from necessity and is characterized by adaptation to achieve a purpose. Pidgin and World English can be observed in specific communication systems with real human communicators, and the projects at the end of the book make it possible for you to begin such observations.

IN ADDITION

As is evident from the foregoing cases, intercommunity intercultural communication is of wide interest. It is particularly influenced by the revival of an interest in local cultures. See especially Barth, *Ethnic Groups and Boundaries*; Williams, *Language and Poverty*; Smith, Arthur L., *Language, Communication and Rhetoric*; Hymes, *Pidginization and Creolization of Language;* Ray, *Language Standardization*; Quirk and Svartvik, *Investigating Linguistic Acceptability*; and Rogers, *Modernization Among Peasants.* Also, many of the articles mentioned in the Bibliography supply specific additional information.

The cases just discussed represent the thousands of communities and millions of persons in the world who, at one time or another, undergo a change in their way of communicating. They highlight three recurrent problem areas. The Pygmalion case centers on the prescription of a standard for an individual. Black and white in America explores some of the questions that arise when large groups of persons undertake to renegotiate and rearrange prevailing communication practices. Pidgin in Hawaii illustrates the inventiveness of communicators when conditions reward inventiveness. Similar cases can be identified in every region of the world (Casmir and Harms, 1970).

At this point, it will be necessary to decide on a Generalization Alternative, a Specialization Alternative, or a Third Alternative you invent for yourself. Before deciding, browse through the cases in the next three chapters. Once you choose your alternative, complete Project II according to the requirements of that alternative.

5

International Communication

The first three chapters provided the foundation for the study of intercultural communication. In the fourth chapter, utilizing that foundation, the problems and possibilities of intercommunity communication were examined, both in general and in three specific cases.

In this chapter, the second stage of communication beyond that of the basic home community becomes the topic of concern. Most of us first encounter the problems of international communication when we begin the study of a foreign language or come into contact with someone who has learned "to speak the English" in the classroom. Again, the problems of international communication are apparent, often painfully so, right from the beginning. The possibilities, if they come at all, come much later and occur elsewhere in the world beyond the classroom.

In the next chapter, the third stage of development beyond the home community—world community—is the topic of discussion.

INTRODUCTION

This chapter is written from the point of view of an observer with extensive experience in world communication. Such an observer regularly speaks the "many Englishes" embodied in World English and, from time to time, communicates in one or more "foreign" languages. He does not minimize the problems in international communication, but he is more impressed by the possibilities it provides than by the problems it sometimes presents.

The central focus of this chapter is on person-to-person international communication. Thus, the typical case is of a person from one nation communicating with a person from another nation. One of these two persons is communicating in a foreign language he learned as a result of formal instruction in school.

The distinction previously made between cross-cultural and intercultural communication needs to be restated at this point. Cross-cultural communication is formal; a diplomat speaking for the record to his counterpart in some other country is engaged in cross-cultural comunication. The staff that prepares a radio program to be transmitted to listeners in some other country is engaged in cross-cultural communication. Voice of America, Radio Moscow, and similar international broadcasts are examples of cross-cultural communication.

International intercultural communication is informal; it is organized by the participant communicators for their own mutual purposes. Most often, the communication engaged in is of importance firstly and almost exclusively to the communicators themselves. It is an interpersonal and semiprivate affair.

Distinctions are sometimes drawn between intercultural and international communication. It is possible for persons who speak different native languages to still share important characteristics of a religion-based culture. Communication between natives of Argentina and Brazil provides an example. On the other hand, two countries that use the same native language—Australia and the United States, for example—differ enough to suggest that an Australian and an American may engage in international intercultural communication.

For our purposes, it is important that we define our terms and use the terms with appropriate consistency throughout the book. The field of intercultural communication does not yet permit terminological exactness. What is more, given the nature of the area, it may not for a very long while lend itself to precise terminological formulations.

A further point bears noting. The nation–state is a relatively new invention of man. It came about in part when reliable *long*-distance communication—the train and the telegraph—became possible over nation-sized geographical areas. The satellite and the jet plane, however, operate on a world-sized area. The question is: What is happening now? By the year 2000, what new configuration should be projected (Theobald, 1970:52)?

THE PROBLEM/POSSIBILITY AREA

International intercultural communication is made artificially difficult by an incomplete, fragmentary view of the area. The problem, almost universally, is defined as learning a foreign language; the possibility held out is that if, at some future time, the learner wants to communicate with a foreigner who speaks that language, he will be able to do so. Thus, the claims about the utilities of language study made by serious people working in this area are often strongly at odds with the practical realities of daily purposeful communication.

It is instructive to review the conditions under which a child first learns to communicate with those around him. Clearly, the child learns to communicate with those around him to achieve purposes. The child does not set out to learn a language. Ask a child what language he speaks, and he will not be able to tell you, unless he has been specifically taught an answer to that otherwise meaningless question.

Language speaking or language learning is an inference by an outsider, by an observer from outside a community. The concept of language is invented by the linguist for specific and valid purposes. But it is instructive to know what the linguist's purposes are and to observe how he operates. Only some of what the linguist knows is directly applicable to international communication—as the linguist is the first to point out.

The Problem Area

The problem area has two parts. The first part is that one normally called learning a foreign language. The second and equally important part does not yet have a name: the problem of learning to speak one's native language in a way compatible with the way the foreigner has learned that language.

Anyone who has attempted to acquire a foreign language in a classroom knows that the process is long and uncertain, that failure rate is quite high, and even those who do well in class communicating with the professor are likely to be unable to engage in purposeful communication with a sympathetic native.

The teaching of second languages is a "big business." Most universities in the world, and many of the lower schools, instruct in a variety of languages. In fact, the smaller the country, the more likely it is to devote substantial amounts of its educational resources to instruction in foreign languages (Rice, 1962).

As is the case for stuttering, there are many theories of language learning. But there are relatively few practices that are utilized on a large scale. Most instruction in foreign languages occurs in a box called a classroom, or more recently, in another box called a language laboratory. There is remarkably little checking of the skill of the learning and the success of the learners when they engage in "real" communication with native speakers (Lado, 1964; Finocchiaro, 1969; Perren, 1968).

There is another side to the problem. Some native speakers are able to communicate purposefully with second-language speakers who "know only a little English." Other native English speakers seem unable to sustain communication even with the fluent foreigner who retains only a "touch" of an accent.

From a system view, it appears possible that the native communicator could use his superior communication skill to adapt to the requirements of nonnative communicators. Yet, so far as can be determined, there are no established programs for instruction in such skills—even though such a program would greatly enhance the success of international communication.

Instruction for international communication, thus, appears to continue to operate on a prescriptive model. Pygmalion is close at hand. The foreigner has the task of communicating in a way and at a level deemed appropriate by the native communicator.

The Possibility Area

The possibilities that open for the communicator who can engage successfully in international communication are substantial. He may study abroad and learn another culture; he may build some of the advantages of "cultural diversity" into his own daily activities. He may engage in appropriate international business arrangements and thereby improve his economic well-being. And he may become a tourist who probes in depth into a single culture and thereby enhances his social outlook. These possibilities are substantial and constitute the major goals for which communicators seek to engage in intercultural international communication.

INTERNATIONAL STUDENT

In this section, we focus on the student who elects to study abroad for a year or more. Our particular interest is in that student who goes to a country different enough from his own to require some preparation in both "language and culture." While many students do some advance preparation at home for their studies abroad, many of those same students require special orientation and instruction once they arrive at their host institutions. In many countries of the world, universities develop special programs to ease the international student into the activities of the host university and the surrounding community.

The Sorbonne in Paris is one of the great world centers of learning. Founded in 1326, it has, through its long history, attracted students from all over the world. To accommodate the growing number of international students, in 1919 the present *Cours de Civilisation Française* were organized. The immediate stimulus for the program was fifty American GI's in Europe at the end of World War I who had seen Paris and elected to stay on at the Sorbonne rather than return immediately to America. It was indeed hard to get those Americans back to the farm after they'd seen Paris (Matoré, 1972).

As is usually the case elsewhere in the world, the Sorbonne program is a part of the regular University of Paris but also has some of the features of an extension program or specialized institute. First of all, the program is organized in a way to serve a wide range of students. Some entering students have no prior preparation in French; others have extensive preparation. Some students seek only to learn enough French to meet a requirement at a university in some other country; others need to develop a sure command of French as they begin long-term programs in law, medicine, and other fields. In addition, groups of students—such as high school teachers of French—come for very specific purposes. The program organization is both flexible and adaptable.

The courses offered in the Sorbonne program fall into two general categories: general culture and practical French language. Within the general culture area are courses in literature, philosophy, history, art, politics, and economics. For the most part, these are large lecture courses. The lectures are delivered by regular Sorbonne faculty. Extensive readings are required. Mass examinations are given. By contrast, the practical language courses are conducted by a special staff appointed for the purpose of helping the international student develop his basic communication skills in French: listening, speaking, reading, and writing. The techniques employed are time-tested and traditional. In recent years, language laboratories have been employed, but the traditional classroom remains the locus for the basic instruction.

The Sorbonne program is among the oldest and best in the world. It is widely copied. Looked at with a detached eye, it includes no single element that is remarkable. Certainly if it did not exist, it would have to be invented, but the sum of its parts is greater than its whole. For some of us who have been through the program, there remains a strong attraction to things French, to Paris, and to the Sorbonne.

The universities of the world are units in a world university network. That network is particularly strong for the great universities in the world cities such as London, Paris, Moscow, Delhi and Tokyo. The full list would be very long, for nearly every nation in the United Nations would have one or more entries.

The similarities among these universities is striking. To begin with, all have classrooms of about the same size, and that, after all, is where the international student expects to spend time. Regardless of the area of study, the information sources are worldwide. However, the special filter provided by the cultural setting of each university makes "getting educated" in Paris different from "getting educated" in Tokyo, even though a course of study, say in biology or engineering, might involve using many of the same books and other informational materials. In the years ahead, the development of a United Nations University will strengthen the present ties among the universities of the world (U Thant, 1972).

The international student, then, tends to find the environment provided by the university to be "less foreign" than other elements of the community. The educational displays provided by a number of countries from around the world at the International Bureau of Education in Geneva reveal striking similarities among the overall structure of education and in the number of available degree sequences. It often turns out that the international student finds things more familiar and more comfortable than he expects. The universities are, for the most part, engaged in a similar venture.

Given the comparative ease of moving from a university in one country to a university in some other country, it should come as no surprise that more students each year study abroad for a summer, a semester, a year, a bachelor's degree, for postgraduate specialization, and so on. At present, of the millions of university students in the world, about 2 percent are studying abroad (Eide, 1970:6).

The distribution of international students is uneven. For instance, the University of Geneva has 30 percent international students, and the University of Paris has more than 10 percent. While the United States enrolls a larger number of international students than any other country, these students are spread across more universities, and the total percentage of international students in the United States is about 1.4 percent, which is below the world average. But the numbers do show a growth year by year, and this growth means that an increasing percentage of the world's population has experience, and for the most part very successful experience, in long-term, purposeful, cooperative, intercultural communication.

To anyone who has been an international student, it is obvious that it is no easy task to assess the consequences of study abroad, particularly for those whose international student days number into the years. But there are some points that need to be restated.

Social status in a home community is closely related to one's level of education. Level of education has bearing on types of employment available. Also, bilingualism and foreign travel are highly valued in some communities. While a student is away, his home community will change a little. Combine these and other factors, and one can predict that the returning student is in for some surprises. He will have both new problems and new possibilities.

INTERNATIONAL BUSINESS

The international student has a counterpart in the international businessman. In fact, the international student often obtains employment in an international business. The skills developed in international intercultural communication are, of course, highly useful in the day-to-day transactions that are required to run a business.

A pattern in international business that has become more frequent in recent years is the joint venture. Two companies from different countries, such as Japan and the United States, jointly form a new company to achieve some specific business purpose. That new company is called a joint venture (Ballon, 1967).

The requirements for the form of business association called a joint venture resemble those set forth for the communicative association we call intercultural interchange. For instance, the joint venture is a cooperative undertaking organized to achieve a mutual purpose, specifically to make a profit, offer a service, manufacture a product, etc. The joint venture is characterized by two-way communication and, in international business, intercultural communication.

It should come as no surprise that communication in international business is the subject of research and study. The success of a venture depends at each stage of its operation on communication. To keep matters in perspective, it must also be mentioned that financing, marketing, and other business matters remain important, but our special concern is with communication in international business.

It has been found, for example, that Japanese and American businessmen tend to employ somewhat different decision-making communication styles. In Japan, the *ringi-seido* decision-making procedure is preferred. That procedure is an elaborate means of seeking and maintaining consensus. By contrast, in America, the majority vote is more often the means for reaching decisions. When Americans and Japanese attempt to communicate, the difference between consensus procedures and the-will-of-the-majority procedures leads to a variety of other mismatches in communication (Nishiyama, 1971). In time, however, when these and other related communication problems are dealt with effectively, business continues as usual (Kobayashi in Ballon, 1967:67).

Within the international business, Howell sees the critical questions of cultural diversity as centering in the area of "people concerns" versus "task concerns." His research in a variety of national and international businesses suggests that the balance between a concern for people and tasks in the day-to-day operation of a business is of primary importance in improving communication (Howell, 1972:B-3). It should be pointed out that the people–task distinction parallels the association–information distinction made in Chapter 3. The joint venture is a dyadic business system. It resembles in many ways the dyadic communication system.

In addition to the joint-venture dyad, there now exists almost every conceivable configuration of multi-national, transnational, regional, and world business arrangements. In fact, Sethi recently collected twenty-seven case studies of international business organization; each of these cases reflects somewhat different patterns (Sethi, 1972). The diversity and variety is rich indeed. Mention should also be made of the regional economic arrangements such as the European Common Market.

The growth of international business is accelerating. The message is quite clear. There are important synergies that can be obtained in this type of organization. In spite of difficulties, including especially communication difficulties, international businesses flourish. As they do, the likelihood that in the future nearly every "job" will require skill in intercultural communication also increases (Miller, Lynne H., 1972:153).

INTERNATIONAL TOURISM

The international student usually goes from his home community in one nation to study in another university community in some other nation. The international businessman joins in a business venture with his counterparts in one or several other nations. Most business that starts out as international—in the sense of between *two* nations—very quickly becomes multinational. The international tourist may go only to one other nation, but increasingly, he will stop in several nations in the course of his travels.

The modern tourist flies in, stays for a brief time, and flies on to his next destination. The big jets have transformed tourism. International air travel, specified in passenger-kilometers, grew from 35 billion in 1959 to 134 billion in 1969. The annual growth rate is over 14 percent. By 1980, the projected passenger-kilometers traveled is expected to be three and one-half times the 1969 figures (Faddoul, 1971:17). In 1970 international tourism recorded $20.5 billion spent by 106 million travelers from 125 countries. The tourist, taken collectively, is very big business and promises to continue to be (Patterson, 1970:24).

Tourism is a leisure-time activity, and the use of leisure by those who have most of it has held a few surprises. Area by area, as the prospect of a shorter work week has been possible, the worker has not been eager to have more weekly or daily leisure. The estimate was that as it became possible for more persons to have shorter workdays, the persons with more free time each day would engage in "cultural" activities. This has not been the case (Girard, 1972).

Patterns in the use of leisure-time activities have included an increasing use of television, an increase in second jobs, and an increase in the longer international vacation. Those patterns in leisure-time use are expected to continue into the foreseeable future (Girard, 1972). There are, of course, major studies in international tourism, and the statistics for any given year, any particular area, etc., are readily available (Peters, 1969).

The term international becomes inadequate to describe educational, economic, and social activities, given the present trends. Interestingly enough, the agency that formerly called itself the International Union of Official Travel Organizations has transformed itself into the World Tourism Organization (WTO). The new WTO will take its place among the 2,500 assorted world-wide organizations, and it will have close links with several UN agencies. The creation of the WTO is but another instance of the two levels: the world macroculture and the local microcultures.

The evidence is strong. Tourism grows on a world scale. But why? The answer is not yet clear to me even though I've taken two trips around the world, lived for two and one-half years in Western Europe, and embarked upon more than a dozen trips 5,000 miles or more. There are certainly the usual answers of curiosity, need for variety, and so on. But these answers and the others like them do not provide adequate explanations. I suspect an important part of the answer will be found in the study of intercultural communication. When we understand better the notions of synergy and serendipity in intercultural communication, we may also understand better why we are willing to work long days to earn the money we so quickly spend as a tourist.

IN ADDITION

There are a number of sources that are particularly helpful in this area. Among the items in the Bibliography, examine: *International Communication*, edited by Heinz-Dietrich Fischer and John Merrill; *Students as Links Between Cultures*, edited by Ingrid Eide; *The International Law of Communications*, edited by Edward McWhinney; *Intercommunication Among Nations and Peoples*, edited by Michael Prosser; *The Passing of Traditional Society* by Daniel Lerner; *Nationalism and Social Communication* by Karl Deutsch; *The Overseas Americans* by Harlan Cleveland and others; and *From Semaphore to Satellite*, published by the ITU. Also, a number of articles included in the Bibliography will be helpful. Additional articles can be easily found by consulting an appropriate abstracting service. Project III is most rewarding if completed at this time.

Three international cases were discussed: the international student, the international businessman, and the international tourist. Literally hundreds of specific cases could be cited in each area and there are several other possible case areas such as religion and politics.

When an area reaches this order of complexity, it usually becomes necessary to reorganize and simplify things. This need for simplicity seems to be behind the shift and subsequent reorganization we now find underway: the global and the local, the world community and the home community. For the two world communication networks—the telecomnet and the transcomnet—make the earlier internation formulations both awkward and inexact. A new approach is needed.

6

World Communication

The foundation for the study of intercultural communication was developed in the first three chapters. Employing that foundation, the problems and possibilities were examined in the topic areas of intercommunity and international communication.

In this chapter, the third major developmental stage beyond the basic home community will be our topic. Most of us become involved in world communication during the later part of the international communication stage. Perhaps a task group is formed, in which seven people speak seven noticeably different varieties of French, or Japanese, or English. As in the previous two stages, the problems are often apparent in the first minute the small group operates. Only when such a group "solves" its communication problems can the substantial possibilities of the group become apparent.

In the last chapter, some possible next developmental stages in intercultural communication are set forth.

INTRODUCTION

Intercultural communication on a large scale remains a new thing in this world. The rapidly increasing quantity of intercultural communication can be documented in terms of air passenger-miles, long-distance phone calls, and by a variety of other indicators (Cherry, 1971). As must be expected, this rapid growth intensifies old problems as it creates new possibilities. Some of those possibilities are both unique and unprecedented.

The chapters on intercommunity and international communication explore a number of case areas. In several of these areas, profound changes are underway. Most particularly, the whole cluster of notions that once rested securely around the concept of Standard English are now open to vigorous questioning by a wide variety of communicators (Smith, Arthur L., 1972). This is a very new development, for as little as a decade ago, only a few scholars dared to question the wisdom or necessity of teaching a single standard language to all schoolchildren. Again, only a few scholars troubled to ask about the details of the style of communication called Standard English. Only recently has it been evident that on close examination, Standard English as a single, unitary target self-destructs.

With the Standard English concept and with many related skills and attitudes, it is an easy thing to display the inadequacies; it is a harder thing to invent better alternatives. One is reminded that the critic has the easier job than the inventor.

In the course of this book, a worldview of intercultural communication has been proposed. Part of the energy for developing such a proposal was generated by my dissatisfaction with the concepts of correctness and standards. In one early attempt, the concepts of credibility (Harms, "Listener Judgments," 1961), comprehension (Harms, "Listener Comprehension," 1961), and attitudes (Harms, 1963) were examined in relation to widely held views of the "Standard English of educated speakers." As others have since rediscovered, the broad questions of intercultural communication are not answered from the narrow perspectives provided by a doctrine of correctness (Williams, 1970; Shuy, 1967; Labov, 1970).

As must be obvious, a worldview of human communication and a worldview of world communication are closely related concepts. As was pointed out, a worldview, or world sense, is a relatively new development (Ong in Prosser, 1973:27). Equally, world communication on a large scale is quite recent; it required the big jet and the communication satellite to symbolize the world communication networks (Cherry, 1971). Not all communicators hold a worldview; not all communicators comprehend that their communication activities form an integral part of the world communication of mankind.

In time, in ten perhaps twenty years, the concepts that seem new and strange will replace or take their place beside existing concepts in the study of communication. One hesitates to predict that the notions of correctness will "die out." Perhaps they shall. More likely they will survive in a revised or an elaborated form. But clearly, if these correctness notions survive, they will have to incorporate the adaptiveness that is a vital part of the communication style here defined as intercultural interchange. The multiple requirements of World English as used in world communication will require it.

World communication, then, is multi-community, multi-national, multicultural, and multipurpose. And it exceeds our capacity to consider easily, in terms of an intercultural dyad or even a series or set of such dyads. We shift then from the very useful dyadic model to a small group model of seven (± 2) culturally dissimilar communicators. Intercultural interchange remains a possible pattern, but it tends to be somewhat more complex than it is in the dyad. Consequently, the problems add up and the possibilities multiply.

As the case studies show later in the chapter, the group of communicators engaged in world communication are most likely to be a "task" group of some type. The small group may be an appointed committee linked by a transcomnet, a conference call linked by a telecomnet, and so on. The group communicates to achieve a well-defined purpose. The emphasis within the group is on processing information directly related to that purpose. The association features of the group are important, to be sure, but they tend to be of secondary importance.

Such small groups increase in both number and importance year by year. For one thing, our most urgent problems of resource utilization and peaceful existence transcend national boundaries and exceed the problem-solving capacity of any single nation. Pollution, population control, and disarmament are world problems. For another thing, our most attractive possibilities of space exploration and cooperative planning are also beyond the capability of any single nation to develop to an adequate level. Space journeys, communication with extraterrestrial intelligence, and the Right of Man to Communicate are world possibilities. The small group communication systems play a vital role in solving problems and developing possibilities.

THE PROBLEM/POSSIBILITY AREA

The two world communication networks—the telecomnet and the transcomnet—have made possible a large number of world organizations. In a fundamental sense, communication networks make it easier to organize a wide variety of communication systems. All organizations require a variety of communication systems. It is in the expected order of things, then, that as world communication networks grow, so does the number of world organizations (Cherry, 1971).

World organizations have the following characteristics.

> . . . the aims must be international in character, with the intention to cover operations in at least three countries.
> There must be individual or collective participation, with full voting rights, from at least three countries. . . . closed groups are excluded.
> The constitution must provide for a formal structure giving members the right periodically to elect governing body and officers.
> . . . the officers . . . should normally . . . [rotate] at designated intervals . . . among the various member countries.
> Substantial contributions to the budgets must come from at least three countries (Hall, R. A., 1971:1005).

Even with this list of required characteristics, there are now more than 2,500 world-wide organizations. Notes that universities and international business enterprises are excluded. Thus, in terms of the educational, economic, and social categories employed in the earlier chapters, only those in the social category are included among the 2,500 world organizations.

Taken together—the world educational, economic, and social organizations—constitute the formidable core of what we have been calling the world macroculture, or world community. It affects all of us.

Problems

Intercultural communication at the world level is new, and it is growing rapidly. We do not yet know how much of this good thing is too much. In a way, the concepts of culture-shock and future-shock signal areas of danger. But what happens when these two kinds of shock interact, when their forces multiply? Does chaos result? Or does some new order result?

In a world business, say in a company such as IBM, that has been operating multi-nationally for many years, there is reported to be among the personnel a sense of being an IBMer, and perhaps by extension, a citizen of IBM, a member of the IBM nation. It is worth noting that of the fifty largest organizations in the world, thirty-seven are national organizations, such as Russian, Chinese, and United States, and thirteen are business organizations, such as IBM and Bell Telephone. The long-term trend appears to be that political units are becoming smaller, as shown by the increasing number of nations in the United Nations, and economic units are becoming larger, as shown by the percentage of businesses larger than nations (Burton, 1972). Where these trends lead us will have considerable consequences for the quality and quantity of intercultural communication.

Possibilities

As the changes we have cited are underway, there is an amount of shifting and shuffling in nearly every community. At a time of change, things can, of course, change for the worse, but they can also change for the better. The basic argument of this book is that the changes can lead to a better world, as we understand more adequately not only the problems but far more importantly the *possibilities* inherent in intercultural communication.

Thus, the defining statements of intercultural communication in the earlier chapters point toward a possible future in which intercultural communication is a profitable undertaking for an increasing percentage of mankind. In a special sense, all definitions operate as self-fulfilling prophecies. In cultural shaping, as Bateson points out, many cultural matters come into being because the members of the community agree on these matters (Bateson in Ruesch and Bateson, 1968:212).

On a world scale and as a long-range goal, we can, if we prefer, move intercultural communication toward a high synergy pattern (Benedict, 1970). And if it pleases us, we can also move intercultural communication toward a high serendipity pattern (Dale, 1971). Or, we can work toward the opposite of synergy, which I take to be a zero sum, hard-nosed competitiveness. Or, we can work toward the opposite of serendipity, which I take to be a sober, tight-lipped concern for correctness. In these matters we have a choice.

In world communication, as the case studies in this chapter illustrate, it is indeed possible for a group of culturally dissimilar communicators to communicate for a mutual purpose. It is possible to communicate cooperatively under extremely difficult situations. Knowing that such success is possible on occasion greatly simplifies the matter. It is possible for cooperative communication to generate both synergy and serendipity.

REGIONAL EDUCATION: EWC AND PEACESAT

University-level education has a special status in the world. First of all, universities are among the oldest of the regional and world organizations. The Sorbonne of the University of Paris, founded in 1326, is older by several hundred years than the nation of France. Both faculty and students come from far and near.

A university typically draws most of its members from the surrounding region. The bigger and better the university, other things being equal, the larger the area it will draw from. The diversity and variety in a major university, then, are typically quite high.

To take a convenient example, let us consider the University of Hawaii for a moment. It is, first of all, a state university. In operation, it is more accurately characterized as a regional university, for a substantial number of both faculty and students come from beyond the state borders.

The University of Hawaii provides the home base for two units which are, by design, regional operations. One of these units is the East–West Center, and the other is the PEACESAT Network. When contrasted with the Sorbonne, both of these units are very new.

The East–West Center has the formal title of the Center for Cultural and Technical Interchange between East and West (EWC). The formal activities of EWC are organized around five problem-oriented institutes in the areas of population, technology, food, culture learning, and communication. Each of these institutes conducts research and engages in training. In addition, EWC operates as a coordination center for students in university degree programs.

The PEACESAT Network has the formal title of the PanPacific Educational and Communication Experiments by Satellite. It has developed ground stations in Honolulu, Fiji, New Zealand, Samoa, and in several other locations across the Pacific. Each ground station operates as a transceiver; that is, every communicator can both send and receive messages.

The term *interchange* in the EWC title is of vital importance. As discussed in Chapter 3, interchange describes communication sharing and exchange and cooperation. PEACESAT "programs" are called *exchanges*. The basic styles of communication in EWC and PEACESAT are similar.

The major difference between EWC and PEACESAT is found in the use of communication networks. EWC employs the transcomnet. Communicators fly in, communicate with each other for a time, and fly home. PEACESAT employs the telecomnet. Communicators remain at home and telecommunicate back and forth across the vast Pacific.

Both EWC and PEACESAT operate in a two-way rather than a one-way model of communication. That shift from one-way to two-way promises to have far-reaching consequences. Two-way communication appears to reduce competition and promote cooperation. But cooperation is something other than the opposite of competition, for cooperation makes possible both synergy and serendipity.

The EWC/transcomnet and the PEACESAT/telecomnet contrast on a dimension of vital importance to intercultural communication. First of all, both units routinely engage in intercultural interchange. But on the long term, say over a period of years, what might the consequences of these differing patterns in communication network use be? Some of us feel that human communication must be face-to-face. After all, humans have transmitted their cultures in this way for as long as there have been cultures. Will a telecomnet generate a "teleculture"? If so, how might a "teleculture" differ from the "face-to-face cultures"? Should further distinctions be made in terms of information processing and communicative association? The list of questions is very long. The answers we obtain will greatly influence the future development of intercultural communication.

WORLD RESOURCE REGULATION: ITU

The International Telecommunication Union (ITU) seldom becomes newsworthy. ITU study groups assemble technical information and make recommendations. ITU decision-making groups conduct discussion in a way that usually results in consensus. As an agency of the United Nations, the ITU has a membership as wide as the UN itself. The ITU, then, is engaged in purposeful, cooperative intercultural communication at the world level. It merits the serious study of any student of intercultural communication (*From Semaphore to Satellite*, 1965).

The ITU began in 1865 when representatives of the several countries in Europe met to resolve problems that arose in the use of the then new telegraph. At that time, there was no mechanism for sending telegraph messages across national frontiers except for hand-carrying by messenger. The operations involved in writing out, carrying, and retransmitting consumed time and defeated most of the advantages of the new telegraph technology. The ITU solved that problem, as it solved many others in the years that followed.

At present, the ITU develops worldwide regulations for telegraph, telephone, radio, television, satellite, and related technologies. These technologies are usually included under the single label: telecommunication. The ITU is the principal regulatory agency for the World *Telecomnet.* Its focal task is the regulation of a limited world resource, the radio spectrum (International Telecommunication Convention, 1965).

While the technical regulations are of importance to every student of communication, it is the style of communication within the ITU itself that is of special interest. And that communication is intercultural communication—long-term, routine, and purposeful (Wallenstein, 1972:367).

In recent years, we have learned that many of our world resources are limited: fossil fuels, food, fresh air, etc. For a long while, the limitations of the radio spectrum have been known. For this reason alone, the example provided by the communication procedures employed are of wider interest than before. And we can be encouraged by the success of the ITU working under these conditions.

The basic purposes of ITU are stated as follows:

to maintain and extend international cooperation for the improvement and rational use of telecommunications of all kinds
to promote the development of technical facilities and their most efficient operation
to harmonize the actions of nations in the attainment of those common ends (International Telecommunication Convention, 1965:3).

Within the framework of the ITU, as it operates at its headquarters in Geneva, there are specialized units with specified tasks. These units are composed of information-processing and association- or consensus-producing operations.

The technical study groups appear to be the key to the success of the ITU communication procedures. The study groups are composed of representatives from different communities of the world. Quite simply, they review, examine, and discuss the available information. At times, they conduct their own investigations. They work at a pace determined in part by the nature of the question under study. When the study group members are ready to do so, they report their findings and submit recommendations.

The results of the work undertaken by several such study groups are then examined in relation to the broad questions of world telecommunication regulation by a decision-making group composed of representatives of the ITU membership—and ITU membership is as broad as that of the UN.

The radio spectrum, as a limited world resource, is of such nature that all who use it must agree to the regulations of its use. Oversimply, one "pirate" user could "pollute" a large portion of the entire resource. It is in the best interest of all to agree on regulations, and to make those regulations binding.

Within this context, a simple majority vote is not adequate. The ITU decision groups work to achieve consensus. When consensus is not achieved, an alternative is proposed, and another, until consensus is reached. On occasion, consensus is not reached, and there exist within the ITU framework mechanisms for dealing with this type of problem as well.

There are procedures within the ITU for changing the structure of the organization (International Telecommunication Convention, 1965:5). In addition, recommendations for change also come from the outside (Panel on International Telecommunication Policy, 1971). The ITU appears to encounter on a large scale the problems discussed for international business. And, as is the case for international business, more often by far than not, the problems are solved. As a result, the possibilities of the telecomnet are open to us all.

WORLD PLANNING: PUGWASH

The PUGWASH Conferences on Science and World Affairs serve as another good example of purposeful, cooperative, intercultural communication at the world level. Their purpose is concisely stated. Sir Bertrand Russell drafted a two-page manifesto that outlined in blunt terms the prospects for mankind if nuclear war were not averted. The manifesto was signed first by Albert Einstein and then by a number of Nobel Prize winners from several countries. The first conference was convened by Russell on July 7, 1957, in Pugwash, Nova Scotia. In attendance were scientists from Australia, Austria, Canada, China, France, Japan, Poland, the United Kingdom, the United States, and the USSR. The discussions centered on the prevention of nuclear war and the establishment of peace (Rotblat, 1968).

The first effect of the PUGWASH Conferences was to open a channel of communication among scientists from the communities and regions of the world. Those scientists in attendance were invited as "private persons" and not as official representatives of an agency or government. The conference expenses were paid by a wealthy "philanthropist" who shared Russell's interests. But the first conference and those that followed were characterized by an unusual degree of independence. The first task was to open communication and through that communication to avert a global disaster.

Like the ITU, PUGWASH is not the kind of human activity that regularly makes headlines in the world news media. First of all, it has never become organized in the usual sense of that term. PUGWASH is directed by a small and informal continuing committee that works out the details for the conferences and disseminates, again informally, limited materials generated by the conferences. It is a quiet operation.

One or two of these informal conferences have been held in out-of-the-way places every year since 1957. Sometimes as few as two dozen and, in other instances, as many as some 300 persons have attended. Most of the conferences have dealt with war and peace for all mankind (Doty, 1971:1000).

It is difficult to assess the effectiveness of the PUGWASH movement. One indicator, of course, is that the conferences began at a time when the "cold war" was in force and have continued to the present time. Unquestionably, they provided a channel of communication. Another indicator is the range of persons in attendance (Cahn, 1971:36). For instance, the United Kingdom, the USSR, and the United States have been well represented at all of them. Cultural diversity is evident. More to the point, the PUGWASHites have been active, most often behind the scenes, in the recently concluded disarmament treaties. The difficult task that was undertaken has not been completed, but perhaps the tide has been turned in this one area (PUGWASH Continuing Committee, 1971: 17).

As the communities of the world become more interdependent, it will become necessary to invent PUGWASH-type movements in other areas too. One such development is the International Peace Research Association. And at this time we need a PUGWASH-type movement to develop a Declaration of Communication Rights for Mankind.

Communication among those who attend the PUGWASH Conferences appears to occur, to a remarkable degree, amid the ideal conditions outlined in the first three chapters of this book. Communication is two-way, purposeful, and cooperative. The requirements for intercultural interchange are met. Synergy and serendipity are both evident.

Perhaps the largest message gained from PUGWASH is that one man with an idea counts. Russell drafted a manifesto, organized a conference, and started a world movement. The movement itself is not widely known, but it does not need to be. What counts are the results obtained, and these appear to be substantial. The critical matter is, of course, that communicators with substantially different cultural backgrounds can solve problems and create possibilities on a world scale when they dare to try.

MANIFESTO: **THE RIGHT OF MAN TO COMMUNICATE**

All of us are involved in a worldwide communication revolution of an unprecedented magnitude and intensity. Consequently, community by community, we find our present monocultural understandings of human communication to be dangerously inadequate. At the same time, we begin to sense the strength of our growing worldwide interdependence. If in these extraordinary times we are to establish and secure the right of man to communicate, we shall require a multicultural approach to our mutual problems and possibilities.

Today when we inquire about the needs and rights of the human communicator, we pose the most basic questions and probe the most complex issues. How does the growth in human population coupled with an urban migration change human communication needs? Does the fact that the major powers control the global communication technologies and world news services inhibit or facilitate world peace? How might we harmonize the diverse needs and rights of the individual, the local community, and the world community? What are the economic, political, and social constraints to large-scale, long-distance, low-cost, *two-way interactive* communication services? Are communication alienation and communication overload likely to be major or minor diseases? Must man also have an unquestioned right *not* to communicate? How many alternate sources of information and what variety in human association does an urban communicator require? What are the long-term consequences of the discovery that information, unlike other resources, is increased by sharing and interchanging? As we enter an era of potential communication abundance, how can we set aside a body of rules and structures evolved during a time of scarcity? Under what conditions will it be possible for persons of vastly different cultural backgrounds to work together to reconceptualize the needs and rights of human communicators who live in an interdependent but diverse world? Obviously this is an incomplete list; each of us can make important additions.

A new conceptualization of the communication needs of man must be developed. It is evident that no one of us is wise enough to conceptualize those needs. This being the case, from the growing strength of our interdependence and out of a multicultural interchange, let us build a comprehensive statement of the present and future communication needs of man.

As we are able to specify our communication needs, we can then move to ensure that those needs become established as our communication rights. For when any man or any community is denied the right to communicate, all men in an interdependent world are also denied their full right to communicate.

In the 1950s, the Pugwash Conferences on Science and World Affairs provided a channel for communication that enabled scientists to discuss the problems of nuclear weapons and the possibilities of disarmament in the interest of world peace. In the 1970s, a similar need exists for a channel of communication to discuss the problems and possibilities of human communication. On the one hand, monolithic world broadcasting coupled with computerized thought control through electronic surveillance threatens humanity as effectively as nuclear weapons did. On the other hand, our mutual possibilities almost certainly exceed the most optimistic of monocultural forecasts by a wide margin.

This *manifesto* proposes that we attempt to work together to achieve a vital long-range goal: to *establish* and *secure* the right of man to communicate. As a first step toward that goal, we must join together to develop a *multicultural* specification of the communication needs of man. Such a specification of needs requires the effective participation of a considerable percentage of mankind. Our mutual effort will yield a set of humane principles, derived from a comprehensive specification of communication needs, to be embodied in a *Declaration of Communication Rights for Mankind.*

IN ADDITION

In this chapter, the topic under discussion was intercultural communication as world communication. The increased facilities of the two world communication networks were cited as a major force behind the growth of world organizations. The increase in world organizations increases the routine need for intercultural communication and raises questions about the optimal amount of intercultural communication in the life span of the human communicator.

Three cases of successful, routine, intercultural interchange were discussed. The first of these cases contrasts the East–West Center and the PEACESAT Network. The second case focuses on the interactions regarding communication regulations within the International Telecommunication Union. The role of the PUGWASH Conferences on Science and World Affairs in the area of disarmament is cited as an encouraging and instructive instance of intercultural communication. Finally, a manifesto is set forth on the right of man to communicate.

A number of sources are useful for further examining the topic of this chapter. Among such sources are Cherry, *World Communication*; McHale, *World Facts and Trends*; Burton, *World Society*; Alexandrowicz, *The Law of Global Communications*; and Richstad and Harms, *World Communication: Population Communication, Communication Technology and Communication in the Future.* A number of articles are also helpful, in particular, those by Gerbner, Goldmark, Inose, Thant, and Wallenstein. Abstracting services are especially useful for finding additional articles.

Complete Student Projects IV and V.

7

Intercultural Communication in the Future

In the first three chapters, a foundation was developed for the study of intercultural communication. The following three chapters dealt with intercultural communication at the intercommunity, international and world levels.

In this seventh and final chapter, three topics are examined that may become important in the study of intercultural communication in the future. These topics are human–animal communication, man–machine communication, and earthman–ETI (Extra Terrestrial Intelligence) communication. Each of these topics stretches our present notions of both culture and communication and promises to introduce a new set of problems and possibilities.

INTRODUCTION

We have come full circle. The planet earth has aged some 4.5 billion years and has a total life expectancy of some 9 billion years. Man has inhabited the earth for only a few million years. Man the communicator has been able to communicate with fellow human beings for only a brief half million years. He has been able to write his words by hand for about 5,000 years and print them for only about 500 years. He has been able to speak long distance by radio or telephone for a brief hundred years. Within the last few years, a revolution in intercultural communication, brought on by the jumbo jet and the communication satellite, have promised an intelligence network, a world brain, of 3.6 billion persons. When that network is fully operating, man will have achieved the full right to communicate with his fellow man.

But just at the time when the communication networks have come to circle the earth, the possibilities of different types of circles, of new and much larger circles, are before us. The peasant living in a remote community, not yet participating in the communication activities beyond his community, rightly considers his community to be the world (Rogers, 1969). He cannot imagine himself living in another community or a nearby city. To the question, Would you like to live in the city? his reply is simply, I would die if I leave here; I cannot live elsewhere (Lerner, 1964). And so we humans often are on the edge of the unknown.

The process of getting to know ourselves has, at each stage, decreased the claims we can make about human powers and purposes. It seems pretty clear now that the earth was not created exclusively as a home for man. We learn that our earth and our sun and our solar system are but one of millions of such configurations in the universe. It seems there are at least a few thousand planets elsewhere which are very much like ours (Shklovskii and Sagan, 1966). And some of us have been to the moon and back. We are no longer, like the peasant in his home community, required to stay on earth or die.

Quite stubbornly, we have insisted that the unique thing about man remains his capacity to communicate with his fellowmen through speech (Burling, 1970). Man can speak. And behind that tripping tongue and those quivering eardrums lies a giant brain. It is that speech/brain link that makes our great accomplishments possible. And yet . . .

We have been just wise enough to discover and invent and create some things that are likely to modify our future problems and possibilities: nuclear bombs and space travel, for instance. We look around us with our electronically extended senses and find some interesting things. The dolphin, for instance, has a slightly bigger and, in some respects, better brain than ours. Notice I can't just outrightly say bigger and better, for risk of offending one of our kind! The computer we have built has evolved through several generations in a brief thirty years. This "youngster" can already do many intelligent things we humans can't. While we quite properly assert that machines compute and humans think, to maintain a sense of superiority, we are moved to word our statements very carefully. Only humans can think (Meadows, 1970). But is that so?

Those among us (and they constitute a respectable number) who are interested in the possibility of intelligent life in outer space have arrived at a tentative conclusion. The intelligent beings with whom we are able to establish radio contact or exchange visits will be much more intelligent than we are (Sagan, 1973). In fact, they may be so much more intelligent that they will be unable to recognize us as possessing intelligence!

These introductory comments are intended to set what may well turn out to be a most surprising stage for intercultural communication in the future.

THE PROBLEM/POSSIBILITY AREA

In the future, both the problems and the possibilities of human communication will differ from those of today. On that statement we can expect substantial agreement. But whether or not such differences will constitute an improvement is a question to which we can expect a range of reactions from NO to YES. As you would guess, my response is yes, possibly. In other words, in this matter, I am a cautious optimist.

Experience in a topic area enables us to discover what the useful questions are and to build appropriate tests. The topics introduced in this chapter are either new to intercultural communication or still beyond our experience. For instance, we have observed that animals communicate with one another. In the instance of bees, we have a pretty good understanding of how they communicate with one another for the mutual purpose of making honey (Wenner in Sebeok, 1968:217). At the same time, we have no clear notion of how to engage in human–bee communication. Bees apparently solve the problem to their satisfaction by stinging us when we violate their "cultural" expectations.

We do badly in attempting to communicate with bees. We do a little better in communicating with birds. With the larger animals, we humans in an authority dyad; man–dog or man–horse, for instance, are able to have a few commands carried out. But again, the communication appears to us to be quite limited. In sum, our experience communicating with animals, in spite of that wonderful night when the animals talked, is limited.

In man–machine communication, our experience is both recent in origin and quite limited. At this moment, human reactions tend to be divided. Some of us state that man–machine communication is on the order of man–auto relationships, useful but in a strictly limited way. Others of us report instances in which men actually engage in communication with a machine and indicate that they "enjoyed talking to that fellow." Within the discussion of this topic, the possibilities of man–machine communication are just beginning to emerge, and it seems much too early to come to "conclusions."

Man–ETI communication, so far as I can discover, is at present beyond human experience. There have been reports here and there in the world that someone has actually talked with a "little green man from Mars" or one of his more distant cousins. But these reports have been received with skepticism and generally discredited. Either way, the claims for man–ETI communication tend to view the ETI as either a grotesque humanoid monster or super-humanoid in beauty and intelligence. Our visions seem quite limited at this time.

In general, we humans have tended to view communication with animals, machines, and ETI as either a bearer of horrendous problems or enormous possibilities, with little linkage between the problems and possibilities. We shall now examine what some of the problems and possibilities might be, what the trends seem to be, and what breakthroughs may be expected.

Problem

The problem appears to have several parts or several subproblems. First, human "centrism" appears to be a major factor. Human speech is still claimed as the critical accomplishment of mankind that sets us apart from animals, machines, and all else. By "sets apart," we, in our immodest way, unquestionably mean sets above. From such a lofty perch, we find it "beneath us" to be seriously interested in communication with "lower forms." That viewpoint is a central part of the cultural heritage of man (Lilly, 1967:xii).

Looked at from a detached viewpoint, say through "Martian glasses" from an observation post in a sky lab, it becomes possible to get a broader perspective on the problem (Clarke, *Planet Three*, 1972:3).

It is an important fact that in every community of the world nearly every child is an able speech-communicator by age five. In spite of the importance we attach to human speech communication, we appear to know rather little about it. We have not, for instance, been able to build a really good talking machine, though we have quite good "number machines." Further, while some of us are able to store speech by handwriting it and printing it, and to unstore it by reading it, many of us in the world have yet to acquire those modest skills. Radio and television simply transmit speech over distances at rapid rates. Magnetic tape and film only introduce the possibility of storage in the radio/TV transmission sequence. It can be demonstrated that the human understanding of human communication is quite modest. Such modest understanding is shown even more clearly in attempts at communication across large "cultural" gaps. We are, in a very large way, culture bound.

In attempting to communicate across species, basically we have attempted to "teach animals to talk" in much the same way we teach our children. The success of this approach with birds, animals, and dolphins has been quite modest. Equally, when something goes amiss in the normal development of a child's speech, our success in attaining the normal development patterns reveals the inadequacy of our knowledge. Stuttering, for instance, often persists for a lifetime. On observing that animals do not speak our language, we have attempted to teach them our language. Only Clever Hans, a German horse, seemed to have exceeded human expectations (Pfungst, 1965).

The attempts to communicate with machines have been along somewhat different lines. Basically, man has utilized fingers on a keyboard as a means of communicating with a machine. Such communication requires skills which take time to acquire. Part of the problem has been the disdain or the awe that individuals express toward the machine (Meadows and others, 1972).

Man–ETI communication has been regarded by man as science fiction. There is as yet no large body of serious and sustained research interest. All of this in spite of the fact that such communication is regarded as an event that might reasonably produce culture-shock of great magnitude (Sagan, 1973).

The problems which retard development in these areas relate to the characteristic we consider to be most profoundly human, our capacity to speak. We continue to regard communication among animals as inferior to our own, even though we know very little about it. We tend to hold extreme views about communication with machines. And finally, we have yet to take seriously on a large scale what may soon be a reality, man–ETI communication.

Possibilities

A better understanding of any one of the three topic areas, man–animal, man–machine, or man–ETI, could be expected to clarify greatly our understanding of human communication. Much as space exploration has made some earthbound problems that had previously defied solution seem simple and easy, communication in systems vastly different from those we now utilize could make the earthbound problems of intercultural communication seem simple and easy. A first possibility that can develop from work on what are now more speculative topics is a much better way of dealing with present problems in intercultural communication.

As shall be pointed out later, the distinction between information and association employed in this book may be further clarified by the fact that man can engage in essentially "association-free" information processing in man–machine communication and essentially "information-free" association in some human–animal communication. What often appears to happen when problems arise in intercultural communication is that one communicator sees himself as seeking information for economic purposes while he is seen by another communicator he approaches as seeking to form a new association.

Some of the possibilities inherent in our future explorations of other systems of communication will feed back into our present practices and may be expected to improve them. Other possibilities will develop into genuine alternative modes of communication.

These new possibilities are much harder to fathom. We would learn new patterns of association, and in an interchange mode, we would develop substantial new information of benefit to mankind. It is worth noting that the horse has lived on this earth much longer than man, that the dolphin "went back to the sea," and so on. The machine, as well, has much to display to us about ourselves. Utilizing what we learn from communicating with animals and with machines, we will be better prepared to communicate with ETI.

I have written the above paragraphs from a humano-centric view of the world. At some point, we may find it a great relief to set aside such a burden. I have at least one notion of how that might come about. Suppose one group of ETI surveys the earth in search of intelligent life and finds it not in the homo sapiens but in the dolphins and the computers!

HUMAN–ANIMAL

Man is *a* communicating animal, but he is by no means the only one. While much that we humans write about ourselves in the area of language and communication stresses our superiority in this area, it seems likely that we will revise our assertions (Burling, 1970). For a time we thought that the earth was a flat plate and worried when we dared to travel about falling off the edge. But as we explored, by a serendipitous accident, we found our earth to be more like a ball than a plate. We appear to be both wiser and happier as a consequence of that discovery. It seems likely that we have a correction of equal magnitude to make in our notions about communication.

Up to this time, animal communication has been most intensively studied as animal–animal communication. In the onlookers' or observers' role, we humans have come to understand, in a primitive way, how various animals communicate with each other. Our conclusions, for the most part, have been that the animals don't use languages like ours. From there, in our characteristic human way, even with very fragmentary evidence, we have claimed animal–animal communication is different from and inferior to human–human communication. But the evidence that begins to accumulate now permits and will soon require other interpretations (Sebeok, 1968; Hinde, 1972).

Our particular interest in this section is in the human–animal dyad viewed as a communication system. We shall briefly examine a human–mynah bird dyad, a human–chimpanzee dyad, and a human–dolphin dyad. In each of these dyads, purposeful and co-operative communication has been demonstrated. If we stretch our notions of culture just a bit, such dyads also demonstrate inter-cultural interchange.

First, a brief note about the mynah bird. The mynah imitates with considerable accuracy a wide range of sounds (Grosslight and Lively, 1963:1). It imitates other mynahs, it imitates a variety of sounds in the environment, and it imitates human speech. Not surprisingly, the interest at this moment centers on the details of the mynah's ability to mimic human speech, with particular reference to speech development in the child (Grosslight and Zaynor in Salzinger and Salzinger, 1967:5). But a careful and detailed analysis of the capability of the mynah, in terms of the requirement of communication, reveals that the mynah does indeed share many fundamental capabilities with man (Thorpe in Hinde, 1972:28). The story of man and the mynah is just beginning.

Second, let us consider a closer kin of man, the chimpanzee. A research project based by the Gombe Stream in Tanzania charts in considerable detail the life of the chimpanzee in his natural habitat. This recent report traces the habits and customs (the culture?) of a "community" of chimpanzees through a wide variety of activities in the long span from birth to death. The story is sympathetically told (van Lawick-Goodall, 1972).

Several serious, deliberate, long-term attempts have been made to establish communication with a chimpanzee by means of normal "human" speech. Unlike the mynah, the chimpanzee does not imitate well. In fact, a chimp named Vicki lived with her adopted "human" family for six years. During that time she was able to learn and use only the words "mama," "papa," "cup," and "up." This four-word vocabulary was achieved only with the greatest effort (Kellogg, 1968:423).

The researchers who have attempted to establish communication with the chimp have been struck by the "expressiveness" of the gestures the chimp employs. From that serendipitous observation has come a new approach to human–chimp communication. Deaf humans rely on "sign" language, and it is this sign language that has proved fruitful as a means of developing a human–chimpanzee system of communication. Perhaps you have heard of the remarkable Washoe. Her vocabulary numbered more than thirty functional signs after less than two years of training. She was able to combine certain of these signs into short sentences such as "go out" and "open food drink." The communication with Washoe continues (Gardner and Gardner, 1969:664).

A remarkable detail of the human–Washoe communication system is that instead of expecting the chimpanzee to do all the adapting, that is, learn to speak English, the human with normal hearing has adapted to the extent of attempting to communicate in the sign language routinely employed by deaf humans. In the course of communication with Washoe, signs not regularly used in that "sign language" have been developed. It seems fair to say that Washoe and her human friends are inventing an interspecies pidgin (Hymes, 1971).

There is a final observation. It appears that communication preferences of the chimpanzee and the human differ in a curious way. For information processing, the chimpanzee prefers the visual "gesture" while the human prefers the vocal "gesture." For communicative association, the chimpanzee prefers the vocal, while the human prefers the visual. In one of the theories of the origin of human speech, the close relationship between the visual gesture and vocal gesture is stressed (Paget in Gray and Wise, 1959). Washoe's success with sign language suggests it is time to reexamine our notions about the audio and visual, the verbal and nonverbal in communication (Hinde, 1972).

Third, the human–dolphin dyad will be examined. The spirit and a few of the technical details of one major attempt to establish a human–dolphin communication system are described in two remarkable books (Lilly, 1962; and Lilly, 1967).

For man and dolphin to converse, it is necessary for man and dolphin to meet in or near the water. Man, of course, cannot talk underwater, and the dolphin cannot long remain out of water. The dolphin has demonstrated, first of all, that he can mimic one-syllable words in terms of number and duration. In this simple way, it is possible to establish a rudimentary form of the switch/share pattern in communication (Lilly in Salzinger and Salzinger, 1967:21).

Some attempts to enable man to communicate underwater have been made. In particular, underwater telephone equipment has been developed so that a dolphin can talk over a phone to a human or to another dolphin at another location. This seems to work well also (Lilly, 1962:61).

Those who work most closely with the dolphins report that the dolphins are helpful and cooperative.

> Our major goal is breaking the interspecies communication barrier so that we can mutually exchange information having descriptive, predictive and cognitive meanings. Until we live with the dolphins and they with us, the dolphin mind remains opaque to us, and the human mind remains dryly out of the reach of dolphin teaching. [Lilly, 1967:300]

Human–dolphin communication, too, is just beginning.

It is worth noting that the dolphin has a brain which is bigger and in many respects better than that of the human. Lilly reports that in particular the acoustic portion of the brain is larger than the corresponding brain area of man (Lilly, 1967:61).

In the popular writing about attempts to establish communication in a human–animal dyad, by Lilly and the Gardners for instance, there is a tone of warmth and respect. Perhaps we are moving toward an era in which we shall look closely and carefully before we conclude that those species with which we do not yet communicate deserve to be called "dumb animals." By our definition, communication is two-way, and while that definition increases our possibilities, it also increases our responsibilites.

MAN–MACHINE

Man–machine communication also lends itself to examination as a dyadic communication system. Three basic communication patterns are evident in such dyads: tutorial, interview, and interchange. These are, of course, the three patterns discussed in Chapter 3. The tutorial pattern is embodied in the student-teaching machine dyad, the interview pattern is evident in the manager-retrieval system dyad, and the interchange pattern is just becoming evident in the man-interactive computer dyad. Each of these man–machine patterns will be considered separately (Harms, 1970:22).

The student-teaching machine dyad is modeled on the tutorial pattern assumed to exist in Socratic dialogue. The teaching machine presents a prepared program of instructional materials to a student. The student responds to these materials. If he responds correctly, he continues. If he makes an "error," one of several "error correction" routines may be utilized (Skinner, 1968:29; Harms, 1964).

The very early teaching machines were quite simple. In fact, the so-called "programmed textbook" meets the fundamental requirements for a machine that presents a learning program to a student. At about the same time, a variety of simple mechanical teaching machines were also developed. But the more recent developments have utilized the computer as the machine that teaches. What the computer adds, of course, is *adaptability*.

Computer-Assisted-Instruction, or CAI as it is usually called, brings the speed, capacity, and flexibility of the computer brain into the student-teaching machine dyad. While the early CAI demonstrations were quite awkward, the more recent developments show a marked increase in adaptability (Kerr and others, 1970:28). As CAI adaptability increases, a subtle shift from the tutorial pattern to the interchange pattern is also underway—as you would expect for an intercultural dyad!

The manager-retrieval system dyad is modeled on the interview pattern. The manager poses questions; the computer checks its data storage and retrieves that information required to provide an answer to the manager's question. The manager in this case may be a business executive planning major corporate projects. But the "manager" may also be an airline clerk reserving an available seat for you on a future air flight, or a technologist checking your medical record, or a student gathering background information for a course project. The human manager asks questions; to the extent of the available information, the computer retrieves the necessary information. As computer networks and multiple data base retrieval systems come into operation, the human comes closer and closer to obtaining for each of his questions the best available information in the world. At the same time, the association between man and machine becomes closer. Again, as the man–machine interview goes well, it shifts toward the interchange (Meadow, 1970:145; Martin, 1969:407).

A man–computer interchange dyad is modeled after the interchange pattern. This dyad is sometimes called man–machine interaction, or man–machine symbiosis, or man–machine synergy (Hormann, 1971:167). This work combines features of both the tutorial and the interview patterns. Questions are asked. Answers are provided. Etc. As in dialog or conversation or interchange, the switch/share operation is very important. The man–computer dyad begins to approximate the human–human dyad in this dimension and in other areas as well.

While still in its early and awkward stages, man–computer interchange poses a number of fundamental questions. Is there any feature of human intelligence that cannot be incorporated into a future generation of a computer brain? If so, how do we know this will be the case?

The key question lies a bit in the future. As the man–computer interchange dyad operates in a way and at a level which is comparable to the best human–human dyads, will we humans come to prefer communicating with computers rather than with other humans? At an earlier time, in working with primitive student-teaching machine dyads, some students preferred working with a machine to working with another student (Harms, 1966:119). Further, in human–human intercultural dyads, the two communicators begin to develop elements of a microculture. Can the same thing be expected to happen in man–computer dyads? If so, what might the long-term consequences be for mankind?

EARTHMAN–ETI

Earthman–ETI communication may also be viewed in a dyadic communication system. ETI, of course, is short for Extra Terrestrial Intelligence. Until quite recently, Earthman–ETI communication was almost exclusively a matter for science fiction (Clarke, *Planet Three*, 1972). But now conferences have been devoted to the topic and reports become available (Sagan, 1973). As you read this line, Pioneer 10 is on its way deep into space, bearing a message from us earthmen to whomever it may concern (Sagan and others, 1972).

At this time, there appear to be three major possibilities for establishing communication with extraterrestrial intelligences: by listening to an existing interstellar communication network, by radio contact, and by direct visitation. We do not know which of these possibilities for contact is most probable.

The first possible method of contact is to listen to ongoing communication much as we now listen to conversation on a telephone party line or a radio broadcast. All that is required is a suitable receiving device and the ability to understand what is received. That understanding may be easy or difficult. We do not know.

To assume that an interstellar communication network now operates presupposes the existence of intelligent beings at several locations "out there." There are some hundreds of millions of galaxies in the cosmos and at least thousands of planets enough like ours to give rise to intelligent life in a form with which we might be able to communicate. If one grants that such life probably exists, one would assume that such life is at different stages of development. Consider how new we earthlings are on our planet, the changes that have occurred in the last century, and those which may occur in the next. In such a developmental time frame, substantial differences can be expected to occur in a few million years. Assume for a moment that we might listen in on and understand a group of intelligences a million years more advanced than we are. How would we use that information? Would we experience interstellar-shock? Might we finally be able to solve the great problems of war and peace?

The second possible method of contact extends from the two-way radio communication that we now use. We are quite able to communicate back and forth from earth to moon. As our technology develops, we will be able to extend our communication facilities. With better communication facilities, we can, when the conditions are right, engage in a two-way interchange. Thus, the telecomnet will be greatly extended.

The third possible means of establishing communication is by utilizing an interstellar transcomnet, that is, by direct visitation. The question is whether we will be host or guest. A few authors have suggested that such visitations have already occurred in the history of man (Däniken, 1970) or that these visits are yet to come (Clarke, *Planet Three*, 1972:94). On present evidence, it appears that interplanetary visitation is possible in the foreseeable future.

If Earthman–ETI communication is to occur, what will it be like? Will it resemble, for instance, intercultural interchange? Will it be two-way, cooperative, and purposeful? Will synergy and serendipity be possible? As you may have guessed by now, my answer is yes. I remain the cautious optimist.

SUMMARY

In this small book, we have traveled a country mile or two. We began by developing a worldview and now find that we need a cosmic view to encompass the future possibility of interstellar communication. We examined culture in relation to communication and now find our traditional understanding of culture and communication vastly enlarged. We formulated a concept of intercultural interchange and find that it can be extended far beyond its human–human origins.

We have also explored a number of intercultural communication cases. We began with the still troublesome notions of correctness and standards in intercommunity intercultural communication. From there we explored the problems and possibilities inherent in international intercultural communication for the student, businessman, and tourist. The next step took us into the area we have called world intercultural communication, and we looked at EWC, PEACESAT, ITU, and PUGWASH.

In this last chapter, we have explored the future of "intercultural" communication. Increasingly, we humans will be able to communicate with other animals, with machines, and with ETI. As we begin to do so, the possibilities appear to be very large, and we shall, of course, encounter a few problems. It matters very much how we approach our opportunities for communication with these diverse and varied intelligences. Our survival on earth and elsewhere in the universe depends on the success we have in this extension of intercultural communication.

IN ADDITION

There are a vast number of sources relating to the topic of this chapter. Look through Sebeok, *Animal Communication*; Meadows, *Man–Machine Communication*; Sagan, *Communication with Extraterrestrial Intelligence*; and Clarke, *Report on Planet Three and Other Speculations.* Then browse through the Bibliography, a local bookstore, and a library. You will find a surprising amount of writing on the future of intercultural communication.

Complete student Projects VI and VII.

Appendix 1: The Rights of Man

Three documents are included in this section. Two of them are complete; one remains incomplete.

The first document is the *Universal Declaration of Human Rights* approved by the United Nations General Assembly in December 1948. Article 27, in particular, centers on culture. Articles 19 and 20 focus on human communication; in particular, information and association.

The second document enlarges on the cultural aspects of the first. Its title is a *Declaration of the Principles of International Cultural Co-operation.*

The third document is incomplete. Its title will be a *Declaration of Communication Rights for Mankind.* It will be prepared as the communication needs of mankind are understood well enough to know which of those needs must become established rights. This task will require the best efforts of a considerable segment of mankind, including, of course, you and me.

Universal Declaration of Human Rights

Preamble

Whereas recognition of the inherent dignity and of the equal and inalienable rights of all members of the human family is the foundation of freedom, justice and peace in the world,

Whereas disregard and contempt for human rights have resulted in barbarous acts which have outraged the conscience of mankind, and the advent of a world in which human beings shall enjoy freedom of speech and belief and freedom from fear and want has been proclaimed as the highest aspiration of the common people,

Whereas it is essential, if man is not to be compelled to have recourse, as a last resort, to rebellion against tyranny and oppression, that human rights should be protected by the rule of law,

Whereas it is essential to promote the development of friendly relations between nations,

Whereas the peoples of the United Nations have in the Charter reaffirmed their faith in fundamental human rights, in the dignity and worth of the human person and in the equal rights of men and women and have determined to promote social progress and better standards of life in larger freedom,

Whereas Member States have pledged themselves to achieve, in cooperation with the United Nations, the promotion of universal respect for and observance of human rights and fundamental freedoms,

Whereas a common understanding of these rights and freedoms is of the greatest importance for the full realization of this pledge,

Now therefore

THE GENERAL ASSEMBLY proclaims

This *Universal Declaration of Human Rights* as a common standard of achievement for all peoples and all nations, to the end that every individual and every organ of society, keeping this Declaration constantly in mind, shall strive by teaching and education to promote respect for these rights and freedoms and by progressive measures, national and international, to secure their universal and effective recognition and observance, both among the peoples of Member States themselves and among the peoples of territories under their jurisdiction.

Article 1. All human beings are born free and equal in dignity and rights. They are endowed with reason and conscience and should act towards one another in a spirit of brotherhood.

Article 2. Everyone is entitled to all the rights and freedoms set forth in this Declaration, without distinction of any kind, such as race, color, sex, language, religion, political or other opinion, national or social origin, property, birth or other status. Furthermore, no distinction shall be made on the basis of the political, jurisdictional or international status of the country or territory to which a person belongs, whether it be independent, trust, nonself-governing or under any other limitation of sovereignty.

Article 3. Everyone has the right to life, liberty and security of person.

Article 4. No one shall be held in slavery or servitude; slavery and the slave trade shall be prohibited in all their forms.

Article 5. No one shall be subjected to torture or to cruel, inhuman or degrading treatment or punishment.

Article 6. Everyone has the right to recognition everywhere as a person before the law.

Article 7. All are equal before the law and are entitled without any discrimination to equal protection of the law. All are entitled to equal protection against any discrimination in violation of this Declaration and against any incitement to such discrimination.

Article 8. Everyone has the right to an effective remedy by the competent national tribunals for acts violating the fundamental rights granted him by the constitution or by law.

Article 9. No one shall be subjected to arbitrary arrest, detention or exile.

Article 10. Everyone is entitled in full equality to a fair and public hearing by an independent and impartial tribunal, in the determination of his rights and obligations and of any criminal charge against him.

Article 11. (1) Everyone charged with a penal offense has the right to be presumed innocent until proved guilty according to law in a public trial at which he has had all the guarantees necessary for his defense.

(2) No one shall be held guilty of any penal offense on account of any act or omission which did not constitute a penal offense, under national or international law, at the time when it was committed. Nor shall a heavier penalty be imposed than the one that was applicable at the time the penal offense was committed.

Article 12. No one shall be subjected to arbitrary interference with his privacy, family, home or correspondence, or to attacks upon his honor and reputation. Everyone has the right to the protection of the law against such interference or attacks.

Article 13. (1) Everyone has the right to freedom of movement and residence within the borders of each state.

(2) Everyone has the right to leave any country, including his own, and to return to his country.

Article 14. (1) Everyone has the right to seek and to enjoy in other countries asylum from persecution.

(2) This right may not be invoked in the case of prosecutions genuinely arising from nonpolitical crimes or from acts contrary to the purposes and principles of the United Nations.

Article 15. (1) Everyone has the right to a nationality.

(2) No one shall be arbitrarily deprived of his nationality or denied the right to change his nationality.

Article 16. (1) Men and women of full age, without any limitation due to race, nationality or religion, have the right to marry and to found a family. They are entitled to equal rights as to marriage, during marriage and at its dissolution.

(2) Marriage shall be entered into only with the free and full consent of the intending spouses.

(3) The family is the natural and fundamental group unit of society and is entitled to protection by society and the State.

Article 17. (1) Everyone has the right to own property alone as well as in association with others.

(2) No one shall be arbitrarily deprived of his property.

Article 18. Everyone has the right to freedom of thought, conscience and religion; this right includes freedom to change his religion or belief, and freedom, either alone or in community with others and in public or private, to manifest his religion or belief in teaching, practice, worship and observance.

Article 19. Everyone has the right to freedom of opinion and expression; this right includes freedom to hold opinions without interference and to seek, receive and impart information and ideas through any media and regardless of frontiers.

Article 20. (1) Everyone has the right to freedom of peaceful assembly and association.

(2) No one may be compelled to belong to an association.

Article 21. (1) Everyone has the right to take part in the government of his country, directly or through freely chosen representatives.

(2) Everyone has the right of equal access to public service in his country.

(3) The will of the people shall be the basis of the authority of government; this will shall be expressed in periodic and genuine elections which shall be by universal and equal suffrage and shall be held by secret vote or by equivalent free voting procedures.

Article 22. Everyone, as a member of society, has the right to social security and is entitled to realization, through national effort and international cooperation and in accordance with the organization and resources of each State, of the economic, social and cultural rights indispensable for his dignity and the free development of his personality.

Article 23. (1) Everyone has the right to work, to free choice of employment, to just and favorable conditions of work and to protection against unemployment.

(2) Everyone, without any discrimination, has the right to equal pay for equal work.

(3) Everyone who works has the right to just and favorable remuneration insuring for himself and his family an existence worthy of human dignity, and supplemented, if necessary, by other means of social protection.

(4) Everyone has the right to form and to join trade unions for the protection of his interests.

Article 24. Everyone has the right to rest and leisure, including reasonable limitation of working hours and periodic holidays with pay.

Article 25. (1) Everyone has the right to a standard of living adequate for the health and well-being of himself and of his family, including food, clothing, housing and medical care and necessary social services, and the right to security in the event of unemployment, sickness, disability, widowhood, old age or other lack of livelihood in circumstances beyond his control.

(2) Motherhood and childhood are entitled to special care and assistance. All children, whether born in or out of wedlock, shall enjoy the same social protection.

Article 26. (1) Everyone has the right to education. Education shall be free, at least in the elementary and fundamental stages. Elementary education shall be compulsory. Technical and professional education shall be made generally available and higher education shall be equally accessible to all on the basis of merit.

(2) Education shall be directed to the full development of the human personality and to the strengthening of respect for human rights and fundamental freedoms. It shall promote understanding, tolerance and friendship among all nations, racial or religious groups, and shall further the activities of the United Nations for the maintenance of peace.

(3) Parents have a prior right to choose the kind of education that shall be given to their children.

Article 27. (1) Everyone has the right freely to participate in the cultural life of the community, to enjoy the arts and to share in scientific advancement and its benefits.

(2) Everyone has the right to the protection of the moral and material interests resulting from any scientific, literary or artistic production of which he is the author.

Article 28. Everyone is entitled to a social and international order in which the rights and freedoms set forth in this Declaration can be fully realized.

Article 29. (1) Everyone has duties to the community in which alone the free and full development of his personality is possible.

(2) In the exercise of his rights and freedoms, everyone shall be subject only to such limitations as are determined by law solely for the purpose of securing due recognition and respect for the rights and freedoms of others and of meeting the just requirements of morality, public order and the general welfare in a democratic society.

(3) These rights and freedoms may in no case be exercised contrary to the purposes and principles of the United Nations.

Article 30. Nothing in this Declaration may be interpreted as implying for any State, group or person any right to engage in any activity or to perform any act aimed at the destruction of any of the rights and freedoms set forth herein.

Declaration of the Principles of International Cultural Co-Operation

Adopted by the General Conference of the United Nations Educational, Scientific and Cultural Organization at its fourteenth session, on 4 November 1966

The General Conference of the United Nations Educational, Scientific and Cultural Organization met in Paris for its fourteenth session, this fourth day of November 1966, being the twentieth anniversary of the foundation of the Organization,

Recalling that the Constitution of the Organization declares that "since wars begin in the minds of men, it is in the minds of men that the defenses of peace must be constructed" and that the peace must be founded, if it is not to fail, upon the intellectual and moral solidarity of mankind,

Recalling that the Constitution also states that the wide diffusion of culture and the education of humanity for justice and liberty and peace are indispensable to the dignity of man and constitute a sacred duty which all the nations must fulfil in a spirit of mutual assistance and concern,

Considering that the Organization's Member States, believing in the pursuit of truth and the free exchange of ideas and knowledge, have agreed and determined to develop and to increase the means of communication between their peoples,

Considering that, despite the technical advances which facilitate the development and dissemination of knowledge and ideas, ignorance of the way of life and customs of peoples still presents an obstacle to friendship among the nations, to peaceful co-operation and to the progress of mankind,

Taking account of the Universal Declaration of Human Rights, the Declaration of the Rights of the Child, the Declaration on the Granting of Independence to Colonial Countries and Peoples, the United Nations Declaration on the Elimination of all Forms of Racial Discrimination, the Declaration on the Promotion Among Youth of the Ideals of Peace, Mutual Respect and Understanding Between Peoples, and the Declaration on the Inadmissibility of Intervention in the Domestic Affairs of States and the Protection of their Independence and Sovereignty, proclaimed successively by the General Assembly of the United Nations,

Convinced by the experience of the Organization's first twenty years that, if international cultural co-operation is to be strengthened, its principles require to be affirmed,

Proclaims this Declaration of the principles of international cultural co-operation, to the end that governments, authorities, organizations, associations and institutions responsible for cultural activities may constantly be guided by these principles; and for the purpose, as set out in the Constitution of the Organization, of advancing, through the educational, scientific and cultural relations of the peoples of the world, the objectives of peace and welfare that are defined in the Charter of the United Nations:

Article I

1. Each culture has a dignity and value which must be respected and preserved.

2. Every people has the right and the duty to develop its culture.

3. In their rich variety and diversity, and in the reciprocal influences they exert on one another, all cultures form part of the common heritage belonging to all mankind.

Article II

Nations shall endeavour to develop the various branches of culture side by side and, as far as possible, simultaneously, so as to establish a harmonious balance between technical progress and the intellectual and moral advancement of mankind.

Article III

International cultural co-operation shall cover all aspects of intellectual and creative activities relating to education, science and culture.

Article IV

The aims of international cultural co-operation in its various forms, bilateral or multilateral, regional or universal, shall be:

1. To spread knowledge, to stimulate talent and to enrich cultures;

2. To develop peaceful relations and friendship among the peoples and bring about a better understanding of each other's way of life;

3. To contribute to the application of the principles set out in the United Nations Declarations that are recalled in the Preamble to this Declaration;

4. To enable everyone to have access to knowledge, to enjoy the arts and literature of all peoples, to share in advances made in science in all parts of the world and in the resulting benefits, and to contribute to the enrichment of cultural life;

5. To raise the level of the spiritual and material life of man in all parts of the world.

Article V

Cultural co-operation is a right and a duty for all peoples and all nations, which should share with one another their knowledge and skills.

Article VI

International co-operation, while promoting the enrichment of all cultures through its beneficent action, shall respect the distinctive character of each.

Article VII

1. Broad dissemination of ideas and knowledge, based on the freest exchange and discussion, is essential to creative activity, the pursuit of truth and the development of the personality.

2. In cultural co-operation, stress shall be laid on ideas and values conducive to the creation of a climate of friendship and peace. Any mark of hostility in attitudes and in expression of opinion shall be avoided. Every effort shall be made, in presenting and disseminating information, to ensure its authenticity.

Article VIII

Cultural co-operation shall be carried on for the mutual benefit of all the nations practicing it. Exchanges to which it gives rise shall be arranged in a spirit of broad reciprocity.

Article IX

Cultural co-operation shall contribute to the establishment of stable, long-term relations between peoples, which should be subjected as little as possible to the strains which may arise in international life.

Article X

Cultural co-operation shall be specially concerned with the moral and intellectual education of young people in a spirit of friendship, international understanding and peace and shall foster awareness among States of the need to stimulate talent and promote the training of the rising generations in the most varied sectors.

Article XI

1. In their cultural relations, States shall bear in mind the principles of the United Nations. In seeking to achieve international co-operation, they shall respect the sovereign equality of States and shall refrain from intervention in matters which are essentially within the domestic jurisdiction of any State.

2. The principles of this Declaration shall be applied with due regard for human rights and fundamental freedoms.

Declaration of Communication Rights for Mankind

PREAMBLE

Article I . . .

Article II . . .

. . .

Article N . . .

Appendix 2: Student Projects

Examine the suggested final projects first. You may wish to work toward a Specialization Alternative or a Generalization Alternative; or, you may wish to invent or create a Third Alternative.

INTRODUCTION

The projects described in this section constitute an integral part of the book. Each project, if carefully worked out, will demonstrate and clarify an important dimension of intercultural communication.

Neither printed page nor film nor lecture provides a fully satisfactory medium for an account of intercultural communication. One learns to communicate by communicating. One learns about intercultural communication by systematic observation of culturally different communicators *before, while*, and *after* they engage in communication. These projects bring you into direct contact with intercultural communication.

To help you and to make a wide variety of studies possible, I suggest you collaborate with a partner. If you can possibly arrange it, your partner ought to be "culturally different" from yourself.

Before you meet with your partner to work on a project, examine the requirements of that project carefully. If you anticipate any particular problem, spell it out, and devise two or three tentative solutions. Convert the problem into a possibility. Work out the final solution with your partner.

The projects are structured loosely enough to permit adaptation to the particular situation in which you and your partner work.

The major purposes of each project are established at the beginning of the project. These are suggestions, not orders. Feel free to revise and elaborate as you and your partner consider appropriate. What you and your partner do as you work through a project must yield information that is useful to you. You may, however, find it useful to coordinate and collaborate with other partnerships or observer-dyads—in other words, to pool information.

Obviously, it is very much to your advantage to secure and maintain the cooperation of your partner. What you gain from your efforts depends to a considerable extent on how effectively you and your partner cooperate. If you are able, for instance, to organize an interchange dyad, you may expect both synergy and serendipity.

Equally, the projects require that you secure the cooperation of other communicators for short periods of time. Treat your "subjects" fairly and well.

These projects are intended to help you revise and elaborate the content of the book. The book contains the outline of the story of intercultural communication; the projects enable you to fill in the details that most interest you.

Operations

When you and your partner work on a project, you form an *observer dyad.* The observer dyad is especially important in the study of intercultural communication. You and your "culturally different" partner will see and hear some of the same and some quite different things—as would be expected from your different cultural backgrounds. When you and your partner combine your observations, you will discover many interesting things about the communicators you observe—and about yourselves as well.

The book is written from the viewpoint of a system observer, and I ask that you read it from that same viewpoint. The projects also are to be conducted from the observer viewpoint, with one major modification. The projects are to be conducted by an observer dyad, as shown in Figure 6, rather than by the individual observer–reader.

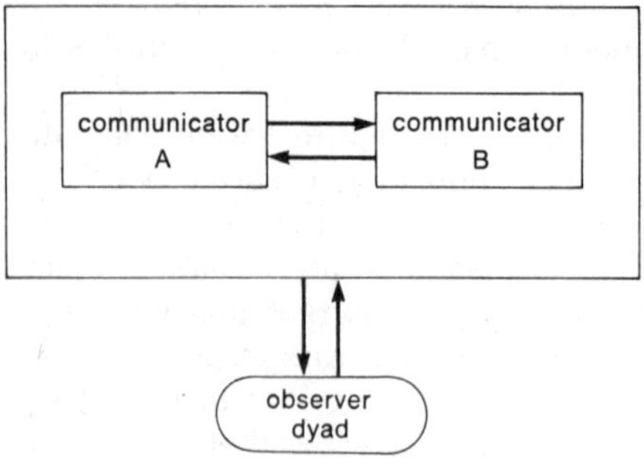

Figure 6 Project overview

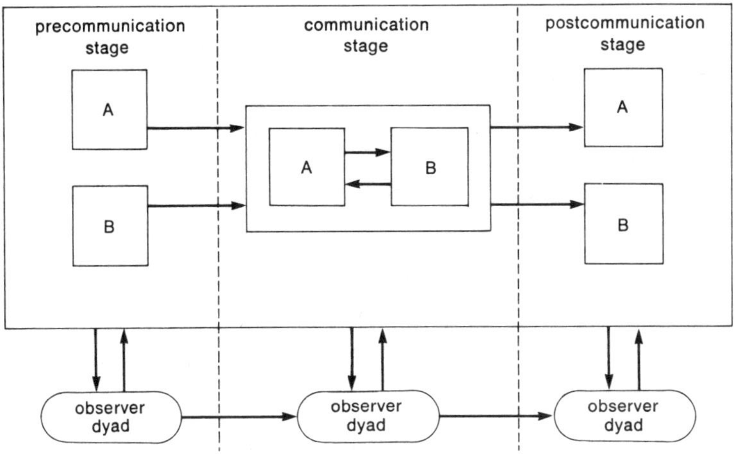

Figure 7 Observation stages

In a slightly enlarged form, Figure 7 suggests stages at which observations may be made: precommunication, communication, and postcommunication.

In the precommunication stage, the observers may administer pretests, measure attitudes, conduct interviews, etc. In the communication stage, the observers may tape-record or film communication activity, or they may perform a real time analysis of it. In the post communication stage, the observers may administer posttests, measure attitude change, conduct interviews, etc. In addition, they may analyze in detail recordings made during the communication stage.

Many additional procedures are illustrated by the materials listed in the Bibliography, particularly among the articles. If you find a study that is particularly interesting, you may wish to replicate it. Replication means that you repeat the study.

Some Guidelines

Intercultural research projects are difficult and important for many of the same reasons that apply to intercultural communication. The individual observer hears and sees those things his culture prepares him to see. The device of an observer dyad composed of culturally different persons can be of help in this regard.

Fortunately, Berrien wrote two articles on the problems of intercultural research (Berrien, 1967; 1970). The second article is reprinted in Samover and Porter, *Intercultural Communication*, p. 327. The second Berrien article, in particular, is important to anyone with more than a superficial interest in intercultural communication. Among Berrien's guidelines, the following are most important to the observer dyad. He suggests that the best intercultural research is that which:

engages the collaborative efforts of two or more investigators of different cultures and countries
is relevant to the questions of our times
is based on a joint definition of purpose
produces information that is "owned" by both (or all) collaborators
attempts to be acceptable to a world community of scholars (Berrien, 1970).

The projects outlined below can be conducted in a variety of ways, ranging from informal to formal. If you wish to conduct these projects as a formal research activity, you will want to know more about social science research methodology. Fortunately, there are dozens of good books on this subject, and a number of these are usually available in a library or in paperback at a local bookstore. For openers, I suggest: Siu, *The Tao of Science*; Webb and others, *Unobtrusive Measures*; Mager and Pipe, *Analyzing Performance Problems*; Bowers, *Designing the Communication Experiment;* and any recent programmed textbook on basic statistics. The full references for these and other related works are included in the Bibliography. These books will provide the tools necessary for starting a formal study of intercultural communication.

The projects are set up for communication by a single intercultural communication dyad or, at times, by two or more intercultural dyads. Figure 8 illustrates two alternatives. One is a small group of 7 $\pm$ 2 communicators. The other is several concurrent dyads that communicate and then rotate and form new dyadic combinations. This pattern has been used in the Hawaii Communication Test (Byers, Coladarci, Harms, and Heinberg, 1971). If you use either the small group or rotating dyads, you will have to make appropriate revisions in the project procedures.

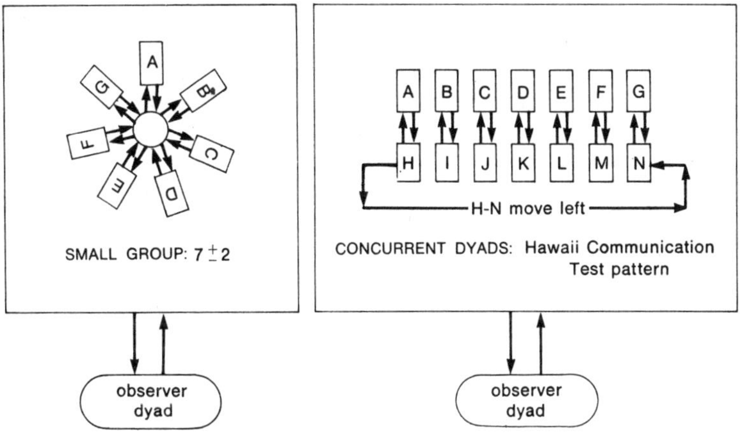

Figure 8 Alternate observation possibilities

PROJECT I: GENERAL ORIENTATION

Switch/Share: Speaker Switching and Time Sharing

Purpose

1. to acquaint yourself with your partner
2. to examine the switch/share operation in an intercultural dyadic communication system
3. to prepare for more detailed investigations of intercultural communication

Background Reading

Two-way and one-way communication differ fundamentally in the importance of speaker switching and time sharing. Review Chapter 3. Examine the research described in Jaffe and Feldstein, *Rhythms of Dialogue*; browse through a book of writings on dialog, for example, Matson and Montague, *The Human Dialogue*; and examine Goffman, *Strategic Interaction.* Also, you may find these articles helpful: Chemers (1969); Fiedler, Mitchell, and Triandis (1971); Gardner (1962); Goldsen and others (1957); Kendon (1970); and Wilson (1972).

Procedure

1. Arrange to meet your partner in a place where you have a small, quiet room available and where you can be free from interruption during the time you make your recording.
2. Either you or your partner will need to bring a tape recorder (or video recorder) and enough tape to record fifteen minutes of communication. Position the chairs and other materials you plan to use. Check to be sure the microphone will pick up both members of your dyad at an adequate level.
3. Arrange to have an intercultural dyad—two culturally different communicators—come to your recording session at the time you are prepared to record them.
4. Ask the intercultural dyad to communicate for a purpose. (Decide on that purpose beforehand.)
5. Give any precommunication instructions you consider important to your intercultural dyad. Write down the instructions so you have them for future reference.
6. Record.
7. Provide any postcommunication information requested by either member of your intercultural dyad.
8. Prepare an analysis sheet. Divide the fifteen-minute time period into three five-minute segments. Divide each five-minute segment into five-second intervals.
9. Listen to the tape. On your analysis sheet, mark in the appropriate five-second interval when communicators switch speaker roles: from A to B and from B to A. Mark the direction of that switch.
10. Compute the number of switches per five-minute segment. Compare the three five-minute segments.
11. Compute the number of seconds' speaking time for Communicator A and for Communicator B in each five-minute segment. Compare the three five-minute segments.
12. When your analysis is completed, listen to the recording again. What do you and your partner observe at the speaker-switch points? Do you and your partner observe the same things?
13. What relationship do you observe between speaker switching and time sharing? State the significance of your observation for the distinction between one-way and two-way communication systems.

14. Prepare a brief report to share your results with other members of your community. You may wish to pool results and make a series of comparisons.

PROJECT II: INFORMATION PROCESSING

Revise/Elaborate: System Revision and Elaboration as Required

Purpose

1. to detect the absolute limit of accuracy in information processing
2. to examine the revise/elaborate operations in an intercultural dyadic system

Background Reading

There is a surprising amount of general and specific information on this project area. For general information, see the following: Black and Singh in Malmberg (1968:105), Black in Geldard (1965: 101), and David and Denes (1972). For specific articles, see: Sigel and Perry (1968), Gregory (1967), and Black and Hast (1962). Some of the references here are quite technical. However, the problem of "intelligibility" is of fundamental importance. If intelligibility is low or mismatches are high, communication barriers develop.

Procedure

1. Arrange to meet your partner in a place where you have a small, quiet room available and where you can be free from interruption during the time you run your project.
2. Examine the Master Word List on page 146–147. The words on this list are carefully arranged to provide a sample of the sounds and syllable lengths regularly used in World English. From the Master Word List, you can construct as many sub-lists as you will need. From each trio of words, select one word; from each syllable type, select one word. Thus, under Column A, selecting one word from each trio, a sample sublist is: way, aim, elk, van, shorn, clang. Lists of any desired length can be built up in this way.
3. Your observer dyad will first examine the absolute accuracy of

a very simple communication task: saying and repeating one-syllable words.

a. Prepare six word lists of fifty words each.
b. Arrange for the two communicators of an intercultural dyad to arrive at a time when your observer dyad is prepared for them. Ask them to stand facing each other, one yard apart.
c. Give each communicator in the intercultural dyad a fifty-word list. Designate one person Communicator A, the other Communicator B. Instruct them as follows: Communicator A looks at his word list, looks up, and says his first word; Communicator B repeats the word he hears Communicator A say. Then the procedure is reversed. Communicator B looks at his word list, looks up, and says his first word; Communicator A repeats that word. Then A says his second word, and B repeats it. The procedure continues until both communicators have spoken and repeated all of the words on the list.
d. As the words are spoken and repeated, both members of the observer dyad individually mark whether they hear the same word spoken and repeated. Do the two words *match*? Or *mismatch*? Thus, under the conditions described above, each member of the observer dyad will make 100 marks (two fifty-word lists), or a total of 200 match (or mismatch judgments. It will be necessary to prepare simple score sheets for recording these match-mismatch observational judgments.
e. Compare the number of match and mismatch judgments in which you and your partner agree. If you like, *predict* in advance what the percent of agreement will be in your observer dyad.
f. If you tape-recorded the 100 say–repeat cycles, a day or so later listen to the tape, and judge again which of the 100 say–repeat cycles are matches, which are mismatches.
g. You may also like to repeat the above procedure with an *intra*cultural dyad.

4. With the same intercultural dyad, arrange the conditions so that the communicators make one mismatch for every three matches, or so that one say–repeat cycle in four is a mismatch. Mismatches occur, of course, as a result of cultural differences between communicators. Equally important are the factors of noise, visibility, and distance. For instance, if you position A

and B in your intercultural dyad standing back to back, twenty-four feet apart, and turn on a big fan, the matches in their say–repeat cycles are very likely to drop below 75 percent and may go as low as 30 percent. So adjust conditions until about one mismatch in four occurs. Then issue each communicator a new list.

a. Continue the say–repeat procedure used previously, but in addition, when a mismatch is detected by either observer, that observer asks the communicators to: "Repeat, please." This instruction means, for instance, if A says *lay* and B repeats *ray*, then A says the word *lay* again and B again attempts to match it. If he does not produce a match, the cycle repeats once more, etc. Both observers keep a record of the number of *mis*matches and the number of repeat cycles required to produce a match. Observe carefully the subtle *revisions* both A and B make in their communication style when a mismatch is detected.

b. Then, under the same conditions, introduce the elaboration operation. When a mismatch is detected by either observer, that observer asks the communicator who introduced the word to "Put it into a short sentence." The responding communicator then repeats just the word in question. If this procedure does not produce a match, the cycle repeats once more, etc. Both observers keep a record of the number of mismatches and the number of repeat cycles required to produce a match. Observe carefully the many details in the *elaboration* procedures of both A and B.

c. Compare the effectiveness of the revision and elaboration procedures. In general, when a mismatch occurs, which part of the revise/elaboration procedure is most effective? Revision? Elaboration? Would the same conclusion hold for longer units such as sentences and sentence chains?

5. With the same intercultural dyad, maintain the conditions that produce about 75 percent matches. Give each communicator a new word list. Then instruct the communicators to

   a. Return to the simple say–repeat cycle used first, except this time, the communicator who repeats the word also *writes* it down. Both observers also write down the word A says *and also* the word B repeats, in case of a mismatch.

b. Examine the number of mismatches between the list spoken by A and the list written by B. Examine the reverse, B's written list against A's spoken list. Then, compare the lists of the observer dyad. Compare the lists of the intercultural dyad with those of the observer dyad. You will need to construct a table to handle all of these comparisons. Also, if you tape-recorded this session, make the other possible comparisons.

c. How many different types of mismatches do you detect? Theoretically, how many are possible?

d. For any particular mismatch within an intercultural dyadic communication system, is it possible to say with *certainty* what the cause of that mismatch was? Please reexamine your findings before you answer that question. How does your answer relate to notions of right and wrong, correct and incorrect, standard and substandard? How does your answer relate to the possibilities that are always available in the revise/elaborate operations?

6. Prepare a brief report to share your results with other members of your community. Do all members of your community interpret the results from this project in the same way?

Master Word List

	A	B	C	D	E	F
	Yea	Pie	Woe	Toy	Foe	Bow
1	Way	Tie	Foe	Coy	Fee	Doe
	Lay	Thigh	Hoe	Soy	Fur	Go
	Aim	Aid	Ate	Oaf	Ought	Of
2	Am	Add	Ache	Oath	Off	On
	I'm	Odd	Ape	Oak	Awed	All
	Elf	Oats	Its	Ebbs	Edged	Ears
3	Else	Oaks	Inns	Eggs	Urged	Ores
	Elk	Oafs	Inch	Ed's	Aged	Airs
	Than	Ruse	Rang	Deep	Rove	Rage
4	Van	Use	Ran	Dip	Rose	Raise
	Dan	Lose	Ram	Dupe	Road	Rave
	Horn	Guest	Sulk	Hence	Band	Gulch
5	Thorn	Best	Silk	Whence	Bond	Gulf
	Shorn	Rest	Silt	Fence	Bound	Gulp

	A	B	C	D	E	F
	Clam	Skill	Drill	Scare	Pride	Slim
6	Clan	Skull	Drool	Scour	Proud	Sling
	Clang	School	Droll	Scar	Prod	Slid
	Coo	Bough	Pea	Foe	Bay	May
7	Shoe	Vow	Tea	Show	Gay	Nay
	Chew	Thou	Key	Sew	Day	They
	Out	Ire	Owed	Ale	If	Ease
8	At	Our	I'd	Eel	Itch	Eve
	Ate	Are	Aid	Ill	It	Eel
	Eats	Adds	End	Act	Art	Aisles
9	Its	Aids	And	Apt	Ark	Oils
	Oats	Odes	Earned	Aft	Arch	Earls
	Tin	Reed	Laid	Yet	Run	Rule
10	Ting	Lead	Load	Let	Rum	Yule
	Tim	Weed	Led	Wet	Rung	Who'll
	Boats	Gowns	Went	Learned	Yeast	Jolt
11	Goats	Gains	Rent	Lend	Least	Volt
	Votes	Guns	Lent	Land	Beast	Bolt
	Frill	Steed	Pride	Stone	Drain	Drip
12	Shrill	Speed	Tried	Stern	Brain	Grip
	Thrill	Skied	Cried	Stun	Grain	Brick

PROJECT III: INFORMATION PROCESSING

Revise/Elaborate: System Revision and Elaboration as Required

Purpose

1. to demonstrate a checking procedure
2. to demonstrate different "acceptance" patterns within and without dyads

Background Reading

Read through a few general sources of information processing: Schroder, Driver, and Streufert, (1967); Goodwin and Holley in Prosser (1973:549); Meadow (1970); *Information Technology* (1972); and Fischer and Merrill (1970). Also examine the following articles: Davy and Quirk (1969), Harris (1970), and Pierce (1972).

Procedure

1. As before, arrange for space, and arrange for at least *two* different intercultural dyads to participate in your project.
2. Construct (in duplicate) a mini-case study, two or three paragraphs long, in an "intercultural" area, such as an international business joint venture or an intercultural marriage. Supply a few specific details. Specify a purpose: the dyad is to recommend for or against the joint venture, for or against the marriage, etc.
3. Instruct each of the two (or several) intercultural dyads: Please read carefully the mini-case study you have just been handed. Notice the purpose which is: ______. We are interested in two kinds of checking procedures that people can use, *while they are communicating*, to find out if they fully understand each other. The first such procedure is *revision,* to make something more simple and concise. The second procedure is *elaboration*, to add more details and make more complex. As you and your partner communicate about the mini-case, one of us will ask you to revise or elaborate. For instance, if Communicator A says three sentences, one of us will ask Communicator B to either revise or elaborate those sentences. When B has either revised or elaborated, we will ask A whether he thinks B has understood him accurately. If A says yes, then B continues by saying two or three sentences. If A says no, then A repeats what he had said before, and B again attempts to demonstrate that he has understood (revising or elaborating).
4. Communication under these circumstances is in "slow motion," with either a "revised" or "elaborated" instant replay. It usually requires a little practice to make the revise/elaborate operation run smoothly. Continue communication within this format until the purpose is achieved, or until it becomes apparent that the purpose cannot be achieved.
5. As the intercultural dyad is engaged in communication, observe carefully the relationship between the audio and visual, the verbal and nonverbal, especially at the switch/share points.
6. Are the *revise* or the *elaborate* operations more often accepted as demonstrations of understanding?
7. Does the revise/elaborate operation work best after two, three, five, or seven, etc., sentences?

8. Compare the two (or several) dyads. Notice in particular those sequences that work best.
9. Based on the successes you observe, specify two or three short rules that can be followed by inexperienced intercultural communicators.
10. Prepare a short report. Share and discuss your findings.

PROJECT IV: COMMUNICATIVE ASSOCIATION

Similarity/Difference: Patterns of Sociocultural Attitudes

Purpose

1. to display similarities and differences in attitudes
2. to display attitude change as a result of communication

Background Reading

Consult the appropriate sections dealing with the semantic differential in *The Analysis of Subjective Culture*, and especially the article by Osgood, "Semantic Differential Technique." Almost any other recent writing about semantic differential will be helpful.

Procedure

1. Arrange for space and for two or more intercultural dyads.
2. Construct a *semantic differential* form, and make the necessary number of forms. A sample is shown below.

Intercultural Communication

Good	___	___	___	___	___	___	___	Bad
Fast	___	___	___	___	___	___	___	Slow
Strong	___	___	___	___	___	___	___	Weak
Safe	___	___	___	___	___	___	___	Risky

Normally about ten pairs of adjectives are needed. Choose objectives that will provide information of interest to your observer dyad.

3. Administer the semantic differential individually to each member of the intercultural dyads.
4. Arrange for your intercultural dyads to engage in purposeful communication for about fifteen minutes. You may wish to reuse the mini-case from Project III, or you may wish to invent a new task.
5. Administer the semantic differential again to individual members of the dyads. (The sequence is: precommunication semantic differential, purposeful communication, postcommunication semantic differential.)
6. As the individual members of the intercultural dyad complete the postcommunication semantic differential, both members of the observer dyad also complete a semantic differential form for *each* of the communicators in the intercultural dyads; they *predict* how each member of a dyad will complete his postcommunication form.
7. On one of the unused forms, enter the pre and post markings for the intercultural dyads. On another unused form, enter the postcommunication markings for the intercultural dyads and the predictions of the observer dyad. What patterns do you notice? Does the attitude of the communicators in intercultural dyads which achieve their purpose improve more than that of communicators in dyads that do not? Are the attitudes of successful or unsuccessful dyads easier to predict?
8. Prepare a short report. Share your results and discuss them.

PROJECT V: COMMUNICATIVE ASSOCIATION

(Discover the "Rule")

Purpose

State one or more specific purposes for the way you conduct this project.

Background Reading

Read generally in the area of intercultural communication Prosser (1973), Samovar and Porter (1972), Smith (1972), Hinde (1972), and Mehrabian (1972). Pick out those cultural patterns you consider most important in intercultural communication.

Procedure

1. Consider the cultural differences that sometimes attract attention in intercultural communication. Some possible examples are: preferred distance from another communicator, nodding one's head and saying yes, signs of nervousness and discomfort, and signs of disagreement. For about a dozen or more of these patterns, write a *rule that*, if followed by a communicator, will be observed as a particular "distance preference," "agreement," etc. For instance, "At all times, *stand* more than five feet and less than six feet from your partner." Or, "Every time your partner expresses an opinion you disagree with, say yes, shake your head "no" and change the direction of the conversation.
2. Arrange for space and for two or more intercultural dyads. Instruct each dyad as follows:
   a. You and your partner are communicating for the purpose: ________. Each of you has been given a card with a rule on it. As you communicate, follow that rule *consistently.*
   b. At the end of five minutes, we will ask you to write down the rule you think was written on your partner's card. When you have done so, each of you will be given another card with another rule to follow for the next five minutes of conversation.

   Please follow each rule *consistently,* but only for the five-minute period that it is in force.
3. You will find a great deal of difference among communicators in their ability to determine the rules being followed by their partners. Some communicators are good at "guessing" rules. What else do these good guessers do well? Observe and record.
4. If you were going to train communicators to become good at guessing the rules followed by the "other half of the dyad," how would you do it?
5. Prepare a short report. Share it. Discuss it.

PROJECT VI: GENERAL INTERCULTURAL COMMUNICATION

Purpose

State one or more specific purposes you intend to achieve by completing this project.

Background Reading

Select several general books and specific articles that appear to relate to this project. Also, check the appropriate sections in abstracting services such as language and language behavior abstracts, psychological abstracts, communication abstract, etc.

Procedure

1. Secure *identical* plastic templates (one for each participating communicator). Those templates used by computer programmers for flow charting work well. Or make identical templates from two five-by-eight cards. Have a supply of unlined paper.
2. Arrange for space and for two or more intercultural dyads. Tape-record.
3. Instruct each intercultural dyad as follows:
   a. Each of you has an identical template and an identical blank sheet of unlined paper. Do not look at your partner's drawing. Using the template, Communicator A is to draw a form on his sheet of paper. He describes what he is doing accurately enough so that B is able to draw the same forms in the same place. Then B draws and describes for A. Then A draws and describes for B, and so on. The time allotted is fifteen minutes. The purpose is to be *both* fast and accurate. Draw as many of the same forms as possible. Draw them in exactly the same places.
   b. After you finish communicating, when the two sheets of paper are placed one on top of the other, all forms should be within ¼ inch of each other.

   Questions? Begin.
4. Play back the recording with the communicators' drawings before you. Notice the patterns of communication that lead up to the mismatches. When a mismatch occurs, how could it have been prevented? By a different switch/share pattern? By different revise/elaborate operations? Write an alternate dialog that *will produce* a match. Use that dialog as a script, and check to see if the dialog does result in a match.
5. Consider the delicate balance between the switch/share operations and the revise/elaborate operations. This balance is sometimes more evident if you write a few "rules" to clarify matters. For instance, write rules such as these for A: "Talk 70 percent of the time." "Ignore 50 percent of B's questions." With a bit of

practice, you can then write a set of rules for almost any speed/accuracy pattern you want from an intercultural dyad.

6. Consider again, in depth, the question of matches and mismatches.
7. Prepare a brief report. Share your results. Discuss them.

PROJECT VII: GENERAL INTERCULTURAL COMMUNICATION

Purpose

State one or more specific purposes you plan to accomplish by completing this project.

Background Reading

Select appropriate readings from among those listed in the Bibliography. Consult the appropriate abstracting services for recent publications.

Procedure

1. Arrange for space and for one or more intercultural dyads.
2. In your observer dyad, *invent a project* that requires your intercultural dyad to invent and create something that does not now exist. For instance, design a new community, design a "________" for the future. Specify the purpose. Specify how you will determine that the purpose has been achieved or is unlikely to be achieved. Arrange conditions you consider most likely to lead to synergy and serendipity.
3. Complete the project.
4. Write a brief report. Share it. Discuss it.

FINAL PROJECT: SPECIALIZATION ALTERNATIVE

Procedure

1. Specify in detail the purpose of your project.
2. Select *one* of the case areas in the book—international tourism, man–ETI communication, etc.—or develop another major case area.
3. Read carefully some of the general writing in this area and several of the specific research articles.

4. Conduct several of the projects (I–VII) in this specific case area with intercultural dyads drawn from this area, if possible.
5. Prepare a report in appropriate detail and in an appropriate form. Your report should deal in depth with a particular case of intercultural communication.

FINAL PROJECT: GENERALIZATION ALTERNATIVE

Procedure

1. Specify in detail the purpose of your project.
2. Consider several of the case areas in the book and other areas as well.
3. Read widely in a number of general sources, as well as a variety of specific research articles.
4. Conduct projects in several different case areas with a variety of intercultural dyads.
5. Prepare a report in appropriate detail and in an appropriate form. Your report should deal in breadth with the general problems and possibilities of intercultural communication.

OPTIONAL GROUP PROJECT: THE RIGHT OF MAN TO COMMUNICATE

1. Consider the possibility of evolving a declaration or a set of principles.
2. Examine the conditions for a long-range goal of mankind as set forth in the *Prometheus Project* by Gerald Feinberg. In particular, how many people constitute a "considerable percentage of mankind"? How long a period of time must a long-range goal span?
3. Review pages 61–62 and 109–111. Reexamine the *Universal Declaration of Human Rights*, and the *Declaration of the Principles of International Cultural Co-operation.*
4. What relationship exists between communication needs and communication rights?
5. Under what conditions, *if any*, might it be possible to prepare a declaration for human communication?
6. If such a declaration seems to your group to be possible, evolve a few principles or articles.
7. What *tests* would those principles or articles have to pass to form a *culture-fair* Declaration of Communication Rights for Mankind?

Bibliography

The entries in this Bibliography are divided into the categories of books and articles (the latter including reports, etc.). In the body of the text, reference to these materials is made in the following way: (Cherry, 1971:72). Where the reference is to a specific page, that page number follows the year, as shown in the preceding example. But where the reference is very general, the page number is omitted: (Clarke, 1972).

BOOKS

Agel, Jerome. *Is Today Tomorrow?—A Synerglstic Collage of Alternative Futures.* New York: Ballantine, 1972.

Alexandrowicz, Charles Henry. *The Law of Global Communications.* New York: Columbia University Press, 1971.

Arensberg, Conrad M., and Kimball, Solon T. *Culture and Community.* New York: Harcourt Brace Jovanovich, 1965.

Arensberg, Conrad M., and Niehoff, Arthur H. *Introducing Social Change—A Manual for Community Development.* Chicago: Aldine, 1971.

Arthur D. Little, Inc. *Tourism and Recreation—A State-of-the-Art Study.* Washington, D.C.: Government Printing Office, 1967.

Bagdikian, Ben H. *The Information Machines—Their Impact on Men and the Media.* New York: Harper & Row, 1971.

Ballon, Robert J., ed. *Joint Ventures and Japan.* Tokyo, Japan: Sophia University, 1967.

Barker, L. L., and Kibler, R. J., eds. *Speech Communication Behavior.* Englewood Cliffs, N.J.: Prenctice-Hall, 1971.

Barth, Fredrik, ed. *Ethnic Groups and Boundaries—The Social Organization of Culture Difference.* Boston: Little, Brown, 1969.

Beckenbach, Edwin F., and Tompkins, Charles B., eds. *Concepts of Communication: Interpersonal, Intrapersonal, and Mathematical.* New York: Wiley, 1971.

Benedict, Ruth. *Patterns of Culture.* New York: New American Library, 1953.

Berelson, Bernard, and Steiner, Gary A. *Human Behavior: Shorter Edition.* New York: Harcourt Brace Jovanovich, 1967.

Birdwhistell, Ray L. *Kinesics and Context—Essays on Body Motion Communication.* Philadelphia: University of Pennsylvania Press, 1970.

Bloomfield, Leonard. *Language.* New York: Holt, Rinehart & Winston, 1933.

Blunt, Jerry. *Stage Dialects.* San Francisco: Chandler, 1967.

Bowers, John W. *Designing the Communication Experiment.* New York: Random House, 1970.

Buber, Martin. *A Believing Humanism.* New York: Simon & Schuster, 1969.

Buber, Martin. *I and Thou.* New York: Scribner, 1958.

Buckley, Walter, ed. *Modern Systems Research for the Behavioral Scientist.* Chicago: Aldine, 1968.

Burling, Robbins. *Man's Many Voices—Language in Its Cultural Context.* New York: Holt, Rinehart & Winston, 1970.

Burton, John W. *World Society.* London: Cambridge University Press, 1972.

Carr, Elizabeth Ball. *Da Kine Talk—From Pidgin to Standard English in Hawaii.* Honolulu: The University Press of Hawaii, 1972.

Casmir, Fred, and Harms, L. S., eds. *International Studies of National Speech Education Systems: Volume 1, Current Reports on Twelve Countries.* Minneapolis, Minn.: Burgess Publishing Co., 1970.

Cherry, Colin. *On Human Communication: A Review, a Survey, and a Criticism.* Cambridge, Mass.: The M.I.T. Press, 1968.

Cherry, Colin. *World Communication: Threat or Promise?: A Socio-Technical Approach.* New York: Wiley, 1971.

Clarke, Arthur C. *The Lost Worlds of 2001.* New York: New American Library, 1972.

Clarke, Arthur C. *Profiles of the Future.* New York: Bantam, 1967.

Clarke, Arthur C. *Report on Planet Three and Other Speculations.* New York: Harper & Row, 1972.

Clarke, Arthur C. *Voices from the Sky.* New York: Pyramid, 1967.

Cleveland, Harlan; Mangone, Gerald J.; and Adams, John C. *The Overseas Americans—A Report on Americans Abroad.* New York: McGraw-Hill, 1964.

Clevenger, Theodore, Jr., and Matthews, Jack. *The Speech Communication Process.* Glenview, Ill.: Scott, Foresman, 1971.

Cobb, R. W., and Elder, C., *International Community—A Regional and Global Study.* New York: Holt, Rinehart & Winston, 1970.

Communication in the Space Age: The Use of Satellites by the Mass Media. Paris: UNESCO, 1968.

Dance, Frank E. X., ed. *Human Communication Theory—Original Essays.* New York: Holt, Rinehart & Winston, 1967.

Daniken, Erich von. *Chariots of the Gods?—Unsolved Mysteries of the Past.* New York: Bantam, 1970.

Darian, Steven G. *English as a Foreign Language—History, Development, and Methods of Teaching.* Norman, Okla.: University of Oklahoma Press, 1972.

David, Edward E., Jr., and Denes, Peter B., eds. *Human Communication: A Unified View.* New York: McGraw-Hill, 1972.

Deutsch, Karl W. *Nationalism and Social Communication—An Inquiry into the Foundations of Nationality.* Cambridge, Mass.: The M.I.T. Press, 1966.

Deutsch, Karl W. *The Nerves of Government—Models of Political Communication and Control.* New York: Free Press, 1966.

Deutschmann, Paul J.; Ellingsworth, Huber; and McNelly, John T. *Communication and Social Change in Latin America—Introducing New Technology.* New York: Praeger, 1968.

Downs, James F. *Cultures in Crisis.* Beverly Hills, Calif.: Glencoe Press, 1971.

Dubos, René. *So Human an Animal.* New York: Scribner, 1968.

Eide, Ingrid, ed. *Students as Links Between Cultures—A Cross Cultural Survey Based on UNESCO Studies.* Paris: UNESCO, 1970.

Eisler, F. Goldman. *Psycholinguistics—Experiments in Spontaneous Speech.* London: Academic Press, 1968.

Fabun, Don, ed. *The Dynamics of Change.* Englewood Cliffs, N.J.: Prentice-Hall, 1967.

Fasold, Ralph W., and Shuy, Roger W., eds. *Teaching Standard English in the Inner City.* Washington: Center for Applied Linguistics, 1970.

Feinberg, Gerald. *The Prometheus Project.* Garden City, N.Y.: Doubleday, 1969.

Finocchiaro, Mary. *Teaching English as a Second Language.* New York: Harper & Row, 1969.

The First International Conference on Communications: October 24–26, 1972. Tokyo, Japan: Japan Management Association, *1972.*

Fischer, Heinz-Dietrich, and Merrill, John C. *International Communication—Media, Channels, Functions.* New York: Hastings House, 1970.

Franck, Thomas M., and Weisband, Edward. *Word Politics—Verbal Strategy Among the Superpowers.* New York: Oxford University Press, 1972.

Freudenthal, Hans. *LINCOS—Design of a Language for Cosmic Intercourse, Part 1.* Amsterdam: North-Holland Publishing Co., 1960.

Frings, Hubert and Mable. *Animal Communication.* Waltham, Mass.: Ginn-Blaisdell, 1964.

From Semaphore to Satellite. Geneva: International Telecommunication Union, *1965.*

Fuller, R. Buckminster. *Utopia or Oblivion: The Prospects for Humanity.* New York: Bantam, 1969.

Geldard, Frank A., ed. *Communication Processes.* Elmsford, N.Y.: Pergamon, 1965.

Gerbner, G., et al. *The Analysis of Communication Content—Developments in Scientific Theories and Computer Techniques.* New York: Wiley, 1969.

Girard, Augustin. *Cultural Development: Experience and Policies.* Paris: UNESCO, 1972.

Glazer, Nathan, and Moynihan, Daniel P. *Beyond the Melting Pot—The Negroes, Puerto Ricans, Jews, Italians, and Irish of New York City.* Cambridge, Mass.: The M.I.T. Press, 1970.

Global Environmental Monitoring—A Report Submitted to the United Nations Conference on the Human Environment. Stockholm: International Council of Scientific Unions, 1971.

Goffman, Erving. *Strategic Interaction.* Philadelphia: University of Pennsylvania Press, 1969.

Gray, G. W., and Wise, C. M. *The Bases of Speech.* New York: Harper & Row, 1959.

Griffith, Jerry, and Miner, L. E., eds. *The Second and Third Lincolnland Conferences on Dialectology.* University, Ala.: University of Alabama Press, 1972.

Gumperz, John J., and Hymes, Dell, eds. *The Ethnography of Communication,* special publication. Menasha, Wis.: American Anthropological Association, 1964.

Hall, Edward T. *The Hidden Dimension.* Garden City, N.Y.: Doubleday, 1969.

Hall, Edward T. *The Silent Language.* Greenwich, Conn.: Fawcett Premier Book, 1959.

Hall, Peter. *The World Cities.* New York: McGraw-Hill, 1966.

Hall, R. A., ed. *Yearbook of International Organizations, 13th ed.,* pp. 1005–6. Brussels, Belgium: Union of International Associations, 1971.

Harms, L. S. *Human Communication: The New Fundamentals.* New York: Harper & Row, 1974.

Haworth, Lawrence. *The Good City.* Bloomington, Ind.: Indiana University Press, 1966.

Hinde, R. A., ed. *Non-Verbal Communication.* London: Cambridge University Press, 1972.

Hoopes, David S., ed. *Readings in Intercultural Communication.* Pittsburgh, Pa.: Regional Council for International Education, 1972.

Howell, William S. "Utilizing Human Resources to Improve Communication," in *The First International Conference on Communications.* Tokyo, Japan: Japan Management Association, 1972.

Hymes, Dell, ed. *Pidginization and Creolization of Languages.* London: Cambridge University Press, 1971.

Information Technology—Some Critical Implications for Decision Makers. New York: The Conference Board, 1972.

International Telecommunication Convention—Montreux, 1965. Geneva: International Telecommunication Union, 1965.

Jaffe, Joseph, and Feldstein, Stanley. *Rhythms of Dialogue.* New York: Academic, 1970.

Jones, Daniel. *An Outline of English Phonetics.* Cambridge: Heffer, 1962.

Jones, Douglas, ed. *Communication and Energy in Changing Environments.* Hamden, Conn.: Archon Books, 1971.

Joos, Martin. *The Five Clocks.* New York: Harcourt Brace Jovanovich, 1967.

Kahn, Herman. *The Emerging Japanese Superstate—Challenge and Response.* Englewood Cliffs, N.J.: Prentice-Hall, 1970.

Kibler, Robert J., and Barker, Larry L., eds. *Conceptual Frontiers in Speech Communication—Report of the New Orleans Conference on Research and Instructional Development.* New York: Speech Association of America, 1969.

Klir, George J., ed. *Trends in General Systems Theory.* New York: Wiley, 1972.

Labov, William. *The Study of Nonstandard English.* Champaign, Ill.: National Council of Teachers of English, 1970.

Lado, Robert. *Language Teaching—A Scientific Approach.* New York: McGraw-Hill, 1964.

Laing, R. D.; Phillipson, H.; and Lee, A. R. *Interpersonal Perception—A Theory and a Method of Research.* New York: Springer Publishing Co., 1966.

Leiris, Michel. *Race and Culture.* Paris: UNESCO, 1965.

Lenneberg, Eric H. *Biological Foundations of Language.* New York: Wiley, 1967.

Lerner, Daniel. *The Passing of Traditional Society—Modernizing the Middle East.* New York: Free Press, 1964.

Lerner, Daniel, and Schramm, Wilbur, eds. *Communication and Change in the Developing Countries.* Honolulu: East–West Center Press, 1967.

Lilly, John C. *The Center of the Cyclone.* New York: Julian, 1972.

Lilly, John C. *Man and Dolphin.* New York: Pyramid Publications, 1962.

Lilly, John C. *The Mind of the Dolphin—A Nonhuman Intelligence.* Garden City, N.Y.: Doubleday, 1967.

McHale, John. *The Future of the Future.* New York: Braziller, Inc., 1969.

McHale, John. *World Facts and Trends.* New York: Collier, 1972.

McWhinney, Edward, ed. *The International Law of Communications.* Dobbs Ferry, New York: Oceana, 1971.

Mager, Robert F., and Pipe, Peter. *Analyzing Performance Problems or 'You Really Oughta Wanna.'* Belmont, Calif.: Fearon Publishers/Lear Siegler, Inc., 1970.

Malmberg, Bertil, ed. *Manual of Phonetics.* Amsterdam, Holland: North-Holland Publishing Company, 1968.

Malmberg, Bertil. *Structural Linguistics and Human Communication—An Introduction into the Mechanism of Language and the Methodology of Linguistics.* New York: Academic, 1963.

Mark, Charles C. *A Study of Cultural Policy in the United States.* Paris: UNESCO, 1969.

Martin, James. *Future Developments in Telecommunications.* Englewood Cliffs, N.J.: Prentice-Hall, 1971.

Martin, James. *Telecommunications and the Computer.* Englewood Cliffs, New Jersey: Prentice-Hall, 1969.

Matson, Floyd W., and Montagu, Ashley. *The Human Dialogue.* New York: Free Press, 1967.

Mead, Margaret. *Culture and Commitment—A Study of the Generation Gap.* Garden City, N.Y.: Doubleday, 1970.

Meadow, Charles T. *Man–Machine Communication.* New York: Wiley, 1970.

Meadows, Donella H., et al. *The Limits to Growth—A Report for the Club of Rome's Project on the Predicament of Mankind.* New York: Universe Books, 1972.

Mehrabian, Albert. *Nonverbal Communication.* Chicago: Aldine, 1972.

Miller, Arthur R. *The Assault on Privacy.* New York: New American Library, 1972.

Miller, Lynn H. *Organizing Mankind: An Analysis of Contemporary International Organization. Boston:* Holbrook Press, 1972.

Milsum, John H., ed. *Positive Feedback—A General Systems Approach to Positive/Negative Feedback and Mutual Causality.* Elmsford, N.Y.: Pergamon Press, 1968.

Moncrieff, A. R. Hope. *Classic Myth and Legend.* Union City, N.J.: Wise, 1934.

Mowlana, Hamid. *International Communication: A Selected Bibliography.* Dubuque, Iowa: Kendall/Hunt Publishing Co., 1971.

Moyers, Bill. *Listening to America*. New York: Dell, 1971.

National Academy of Engineering. *Reports on Selected Topics in Telecommunication*. Washington, D.C.: National Academy of Sciences, 1969.

Nelson, James. *Wisdom for Our Time*. New York: Norton, 1961.

Nylen, Donald; Mitchell, J. Robert; and Stout, Anthony. *Handbook of Staff Development and Human Relations Training: Materials Developed for Use in Africa*. Washington, D.C.: National Training Laboratories Institute for Applied Behavioral Science, associated with NEA, 1967.

Office of International Investment. *The Multinational Corporation—Studies on U.S. Foreign Investment*. Washington, D.C.: Government Printing Office, March 1972.

Oliver, Robert T. *Communication and Culture in Ancient India and China*. Syracuse, N.Y.: Syracuse University Press, 1971.

Oliver, Robert T. *Culture and Communication—The Problem of Penetrating National and Cultural Boundaries*. Springfield, Ill.: C. C Thomas, 1962.

Owen, Wilfred. *The Accessible City*. Washington, D.C.: Brookings, 1972.

Perren, G. E., ed. *Teachers of English as a Second Language—Their Training and Preparation*. London: Cambridge University Press, 1968.

Peters, Michael. *International Tourism—The Economics and Development of the International Tourist Trade*. London: Hutchinson, 1969.

Pfungst, Oskar. *Clever Hans (The Horse of Mr. Von Osten)*. New York: Holt, Rinehart & Winston, 1965.

Pinkney, Alphonso. *Black Americans*. Englewood Cliffs, N.J.: Prentice-Hall, 1969.

Prosser, Michael H., ed. *Intercommunication Among Nations and Peoples*. New York: Harper & Row, 1973.

Quirk, Randolph. *The Use of English*. New York: St. Martin, 1962.

Quirk, Randolph, and Svartvik, Jan. *Investigating Linguistic Acceptability*. The Hague: Mouton & Co., 1966.

Random House Dictionary of the English Language, Unabridged Edition. New York: Random House, 1966.

Rao, Y. V. Lakshmana. *Communication and Development—A Study of Two Indian Villages*. Minneapolis, Minn.: University of Minnesota Press, 1966.

Ray, Punya Sloka. *Language Standardization—Studies in Prescriptive Linguistics*. The Hague: Mouton and Company, 1963.

Remer, Theodore G., ed. *Serendipity and the Three Princes—From the Peregrinaggio of 1557*. Norman, Okla.: University of Oklahoma Press, 1965.

Rice, Frank A., ed. *Study of the Role of Second Languages in Asia, Africa, and Latin America.* Washington, D.C.: Center for Applied Linguistics of the Modern Language Association of America, 1962.

Richstad, Jim A., and Harms, L. S., eds. *World Communication: Population Communication, Communication Technology, and Communication in the Future.* Honolulu: East-West Center, 1973.

Rogers, E. M. *Modernization Among Peasants—The Impact of Communication.* New York: Holt, Rinehart & Winston, 1969.

Rogers, E. M., and Shoemaker, F. F. *Communication of Innovations.* New York: Free Press, 1971.

Rose, Caroline B. *Sociology: The Study of Man in Society.* Columbus, Ohio: Merrill, 1965.

Rosenthal, Robert, and Jacobson, Lenore. *Pygmalion in the Classroom—Teacher Expectation and Pupil's Intellectual Development.* New York: Holt, Rinehart & Winston, 1968.

Roslansky, John D., ed. *Communication—A Discussion at the Nobel Conference.* Amsterdam: North Holland Publishing Company, 1969.

Rotblat, J. *Pugwash—The First Ten Years: History of the Conferences of Science and World Affairs.* New York: Humanities, 1968.

Ruesch, J., and Bateson, G. *Communication: The Social Matrix of Psychiatry.* New York: Norton, 1968.

Russell, Bertrand. *Has Man a Future?* Baltimore, Md.: Penguin, 1961.

Ruzic, Neil P. *Where the Winds Sleep.* Garden City, New York: Doubleday, 1970.

Sagan, Carl, ed. *Communication with Extraterrestrial Intelligence.* Cambridge, Mass.: The M.I.T. Press, 1973.

Salzinger, Kurt, and Salzinger, Suzanne, eds. *Research in Verbal Behavior and Some Neurophysiological Implications.* New York: Academic, 1967.

Samovar, Larry A., and Porter, Richard E., *Intercultural Communication: A Reader.* Belmont, Calif.: Wadsworth Publishing Co., 1972.

Schramm, Wilbur. *Mass Media and National Development—The Role of Information in the Developing Countries.* Stanford, Calif.: Stanford University Press, 1964.

Schroder, Harold M.; Driver, Michael J.; and Streufert, Siegfried. *Human Information Processing—Individuals and Groups Functioning in Complex Social Situations.* New York: Holt, Rinehart & Winston, 1967.

Sebeok, Thomas A., ed. *Animal Communication—Techniques of Study and Results of Research.* Bloomington, Ind.: Indiana University Press, 1968.

Segall, Marshall H.; Campbell, Donald T.; and Herskovits, Melville J. *The Influence of Culture on Visual Perception.* Indianapolis, Ind.: Bobbs-Merrill, 1966.

Sereno, Kenneth K., and Mortensen, C. David, eds. *Foundations of Communication Theory.* New York: Harper & Row, 1970.

Sethi, S. Prakash. *Advanced Cases in Multinational Business Operations.* Pacific Palisades, Calif.: Goodyear Publishing Co., 1972.

Shaw, George Bernard. *Selected Plays.* New York: Dodd, Mead, 1948.

Shklovskii, I. S., and Sagan, Carl. *Intelligent Life in the Universe.* New York: Dell, 1966.

Shuy, Roger W. *Discovering American Dialects.* Champaign, Ill.: National Council of Teachers of English, 1967.

Siegman, A. W., and Pope, B., eds. *Studies in Dyadic Communication.* Elmsford, New York: Pergamon, 1972.

Siu, R. G. H. *The Tao of Science.* Cambridge: M.I.T. Press, 1957.

Skinner, B. F. *The Technology of Teaching.* New York: Appleton-Century-Crofts, 1968.

Smith, Alfred, ed. *Communication and Culture—Readings in the Code of Human Interaction.* New York: Holt, Rinehart & Winston, 1966.

Smith, Arthur L. *Language, Communication and Rhetoric in Black America.* New York: Harper & Row, 1972.

Smith, Ralph Lee. *The Wired Nation.* New York: Harper & Row, 1972.

Snow, C. P. *The Two Cultures: And A Second Look.* New York: New American Library, 1963.

Sommer, Robert. *Personal Space—The Behavioral Basis of Design.* Englewood Cliffs, N.J.: Prentice-Hall, 1969.

Spencer, John, ed. *Language in Africa.* London: Cambridge University Press, 1963.

Steinberg, Charles S., ed. *Mass Media and Communication.* New York: Hastings House, 1972.

Stewart, Harold. *A Net of Fireflies: An Anthology of 320 Japanese Haiku Translated into English Verse.* Rutland, Vermont: Tuttle, 1960.

Swanson, Bert E. *The Concern for Community in Urban America.* New York: Odyssey, 1970.

Swift, Jonathan. *Gulliver's Travels.* New York: Holt, Rinehart & Winston, 1954.

Textor, Robert B., ed. *Cultural Frontiers of the Peace Corps.* Cambridge, Mass.: The M.I.T. Press, 1966.

Theobald, Robert. *An Alternative Future for America II.* Denver, Col.: Swallow, 1970.

Toffler, Alvin. *Future Shock.* New York: Bantam, 1971.

Trager, George L. *Language and Languages.* San Francisco: Chandler, 1972.

Triandis, Harry C. *The Analysis of Subjective Culture.* New York: Wiley, 1972.

Twentieth Century Fund Task Force Report. *Communicating by Satellite.* New York: Twentiety Century, 1969.

Twentieth Century Fund Task Force Report. *The Future of Satellite Communications.* New York: Twentieth Century, 1970.

van Lawick-Goodall, Jane. *In the Shadow of Man.* New York: Dell, 1972.

Vernon, Raymond. *The Economic and Political Consequences of Multinational Enterprise: An Anthology.* Boston: Harvard Business School, Division of Research, 1972.

Watzlawick, P.; Beavin, J. H.; and Jackson, D. D. *Pragmatics of Human Communication.* New York: W. W. Norton and Company, 1967.

Webb, Eugene J., and others. *Unobtrusive Measures: Non-reactive Research in the Social Sciences.* Skokie, Ill.: Rand McNally, 1967.

Weinstein, G., and Fantini, M. D. *Toward Humanistic Education: A Curriculum of Affect.* New York: Praeger, 1970.

Williams, Frederick, ed. *Language and Poverty—Perspectives on a Theme.* Chicago, Markham Publishing Co., 1970.

ARTICLES

Abate, Mario, and Berrien, F. K. "Validation of Stereotypes: Japanese Versus American Students." *Journal of Personality and Social Psychology* 7, no. 4 (1967):435–438.

Ajiferuke, Musbau, and Boddewyn, J. " 'Culture' and other Explanatory Variables in Comparative Management Studies." *Academy of Management Journal* 13 (1970):153–163.

Atkeson, Paula. "Building Communication in Intercultural Marriage." *Psychiatry* 33 (1970):396–408.

Benedict, Ruth "Synergy: Patterns of the Good Culture." *Psychology Today*, June 1970:78

Berrien, F. Kenneth. "Methodological and Related Problems in Cross-Cultural Research." *International Journal of Psychology* 2 (1967):33–43.

Berrien, F. Kenneth. "A Super-Ego for Cross-Cultural Research." *International Journal of Psychology* 5 (1970):33–39.

Black, John W., and Hast, Malcolm H. "Speech Reception with Altering Signal." *Journal of Speech and Hearing Research* 5 (1962):70–75.

Bohannan, Paul. "Our Two-Story Culture." *Saturday Review* (September 1972), pp. 40–41.

Brooks, Nelson. "A Guest Editorial: Culture—A New Frontier." *Foreign Language Annals* 3 (1971):54–61.

Byers, Burton; Coladarci, Arthur; Harms, L. S.; and Heinberg, Paul. "The Hawaii Communication Test." Honolulu: State Department of Education, 1971.

Byrne, Donn, and Andres, David. "Prejudice and Interpersonal Expectancies." *The Journal of Negro Education* 33 (1964):441–445.

Byrne, Donn, and Clore, Gerald L., Jr. "Predicting Interpersonal Attraction Toward Strangers Presented in Three Different Stimulus Modes." *Psychonomic Science* 4, no. 6 (1966):239–240.

Byrne, Donn; Griffitt, William; and Stefaniak, Daniel. "Attraction and Similarity of Personality Characteristics." *Journal of Personality and Social Psychology* 5, no. 1 (1967):82–90.

Byrne, Donn, and Wong, Terry J. "Racial Prejudice, Interpersonal Attraction, and Assumed Dissimilarity of Attitudes." *Journal of Abnormal and Social Psychology* 65, no. 4 (1962):246–253.

Bystrom, John. "The Peacesat Project." A Report for the International Communication Association. University of Hawaii, Speech-Communication Department, 1972.

Cahn, Anne H. "A Student's View of Pugwash." *Bulletin of the Atomic Scientists* (April 1971):36–37.

Chaiklin, Joseph B. "Native American Listener's Adaptation in Understanding Speakers with Foreign Dialect." *Journal of Speech and Hearing Disorders* 13:165–170.

Chemers, Martin M. "Cross-Cultural Training as a Means for Improving Situational Favorableness." *Human Relations* 22 (1969):531–546.

Cole, Michael, et al. "A Cross-Cultural Investigation of Information Processing." *International Journal of Psychology* 3 (1968):93–102.

Cook, Vivian J. "The Analogy Between First and Second Language Learning." *International Review of Applied Linguistics* 7 (1969):207–216.

Cultural Policy: A Preliminary Study. Paris: UNESCO, 1969.

Curran, Charles A. "Counseling Skills Adapted to the Learning of Foreign Languages." *Bulletin of the Menninger Clinic* 25, no. 2 (1961):78–93.

Dale, Edgar. "Serendipity." *The News Letter* 36, no. 5 (1971):1–4.

Dance, Frank E. X. "The 'Concept' of Communication." *The Journal of Communication* 20 (1970):201–210.

d'Arcy, Jean. "Direct Broadcast Satellites and the Right to Communicate." *EBU Review* 118 (1969):14–18.

Davy, Derek, and Quirk, Randolph. "An Acceptability Experiment with Spoken Output." *Journal of Linguistics* 5 (1969):109–120.

Deutsch, Steven E., and Won, George Y. M. "Some Factors in the Adjustment of Foreign Nationals in the United States." *Journal of Social Issues* 19 (1963):115–122.

"Disarmament and Arms Limitation: Pugwash Assessment." *Bulletin of the Atomic Scientists* (March 1971):20–23.

Doty, Paul. "The Community of Science and the Search for Peace." *Science* 173 (1971):998–1002.

Eisenberg, Leon. "The *Human* Nature of Human Nature." *Science* 176 (1972):123–128.

Ekman, Paul; Sorenson, E. Richard; and Friesen, Wallace V. "Pan-Cultural Elements in Facial Displays of Emotion." '*Science* 164 (1969):86–88.

Ellingsworth, Huber W. "Training Teachers and Technicians as Change Agents—A Communication Approach." *International Programs*, pp. 1–7, Michigan State University, 1966.

Emerson, Thomas I. "Communication and Freedom of Expression." *Scientific American* 227, no. 3 (1972):163–172.

Faddoul, Georges. "The Development of Tourism and Air Transport." *World Travel* 98/99 (1971):17–20.

Feenstra, H. J. "The Process of Second-Language Learning." *Proceedings of the 16th Congress of Applied Psychology* 4 (1968):576–584.

Ferguson, Charles A. "Myths About Arabic." *Monograph Series on Languages and Linguistics* 12 (1959):75–82.

Fiedler, Fred E.; Mitchell, Terence; and Triandis, Harry C. "The Culture Assimilator: An Approach to Cross-Cultural Training." *Journal of Applied Psychology* 55, no. 2 (1971):95–102.

Fishman, Joshua A. "Socio-linguistics and the Language Problems of the Developing Countries." *International Social Science Journal* 20 (1968): 211–225.

Gardner, George H. "Cross Cultural Communication." *Journal of Social Psychology* 58 (1962):241–251.

Gardner, R. Allen and Beatrice T. "Teaching Sign Language to a Chimpanzee." *Science* 165 (1969):664–672.

Gardner, R. C., and Lambert, W. E. "Language Aptitude, Intelligence and Second-Language Achievement." *Journal of Educational Psychology* 56 (1965):191–199.

Garner, John E., and Schutz, Noel W., Jr. "The 'Missing Link' in our English Instruction." *Journal of English as a Second Language* 4 (1969): 35–45.

Gerbner, George. "Communication and Social Environment." *Scientific American* 227, no. 3 (1972):152–160.

Harms, L. S. "Interchange in Speech Communication." *Proceedings of the Sixth International Congress of Phonetic Sciences*, Prague, 1970:425–428.

Harms, L. S. "Listener Comprehension of Speakers of Three Status Groups." *Language and Speech* 4, part 2 (1961):109–112.

Harms, L. S. "Listener Judgments of Status Cues in Speech." *Quarterly Journal of Speech* 47 (1961):164–168.

Harms, L. S. "Social Dialect and Speech Communication Proficiency." *Actes Du Xe Congrès International Des Linguistes, Bucarest*, 1969:663–668.

Heinberg, Paul; Harms, L. S.; and Yamada, June. "Speech–Communication Learning System, Volumes I and II." Honolulu: International Learning Systems, 1969, 1970.

Hormann, Aiko M. "A Man–Machine Synergistic Approach to Planning and Creative Problem Solving, Part I." *International Journal of Man-Machine Studies* 3 (1971):167–184, 241–267.

Inkeles, Alex, and Smith, David H. "The Fate of Personal Adjustment in the Process of Modernization." *International Journal of Comparative Sociology* 11, no. 2 (1970):81–114.

Inose, Hiroshi. "Communication Networks." *Scientific American* 227, no. 3 (1972):116–128.

"The International Telecommunication Union: Issues and Next Steps." Report by the Panel on International Telecommunications Policy. New York: Carnegie Endowment, 1971.

"IUOTO Holds Its XXIInd General Assembly at Ankara." *World Travel* 103 (1971):3–5.

Kellogg, Winthrop N. "Communication and Language in the Home-Raised Chimpanzee." *Science* 162 (1968):423–427.

Kendon, Adam. "Movement Coordination in Social Interaction: Some Examples Described." *Acta Psychologica* 32 (1970):100–125.

Kerr, Eugene G., and others. "An Instructional System for Computer Assisted Instruction on a General Purpose Computer." *Educational Technology* 10, no. 3 (1970):28–30.

Khubchandani, Lachman M. "Language Planning in a Multilingual Communication Network: Certain Basic Assumptions." Proceedings of the Xth International Congress of Linguistics, Bucarest, 1969.

Kimple, James, and others. "Language Switching and the Interpretation of Conversations." *Lingua* 23 (1969):127–134.

Kirk, Paul L. "Dialect Intelligibility Testing: The Mazatec Study." *International Journal of American Linguistics* 36 (1970):205–211.

Lado, Robert. "Memory Span as a Factor in Second Language Learning." *International Review of Applied Linguistics* 3 (1965):123–129.

Lambert, Wallace E. "Developmental Aspects of Second-Language Acquisition, I." *Journal of Social Psychology* 43 (1956):83–89.

Lambert, Wallace E. "Developmental Aspects of Second-Language Acquisition, II." *Journal of Social Psychology* 43 (1956):91–98.

Lambert, Wallace E. "Developmental Aspects of Second-Language Acquisition, III." *Journal of Social Psychology* 43 (1956):99–104.

Lane, Harlan. "Foreign Accent and Speech Distortion." *Journal of the Acoustical Society of America* 35, no. 4 (1963):451–453.

Lilly, John C. "Vocal Mimicry in Turisops: Ability to Match Numbers and Durations of Human Vocal Bursts." *Science* 147 (1965):300–301.

Lomax, Alan, and Berkowitz, Norman. "The Evolutionary Taxonomy of Culture." *Science* 177 (1972):228–239.

Malek-Asghar, M. "Venice Plan 1971—Interregional Telecommunication Network." *ITU Telecommunication Journal* (May 1972):1–12.

Maslow, Abraham H., and Honigmann, John J., eds. "Synergy: Some Notes of Ruth Benedict." *American Anthropologist* 72 (1970):320–333.

Matoré, Georges. Personal interview, 18 July 1972.

"Meetings—The 21st Pugwash Conference on Science and World Affairs." *Science* 174 (1971):1150–1156.

Meredith, Gerald M. "Amae and Acculturation Among Japanese–American College Students in Hawaii." *Journal of Social Psychology* 70 (1966): 171–180.

Moussa, Sayed A. "The Tourist Image." *World Travel* 101 (1971):31.

Murphy, H. B. M. "Social Action by Singapore Chinese High School Students." Presented at the Conference on Culture and Mental Health in Asia and the Pacific. Honolulu: Social Science Research Institute and East-West Center, 1961.

Nayar, E. S. K., et al. "Training, Task, and Mediator Orientation in Heterocultural Negotiations." *Human Relations* 21:283–294.

Nichols, Alan C. "Apparent Factors Leading to Errors in Audition Made by Foreign Students." *Speech Monographs* 31 (1964):85–91.

Nida, Eugene A., and Fehderau, Harold W. "Indigenous Pidgins and Koines." *International Journal of American Linguistics* 36 (1970):146–155.

Nishiyama, Kazuo. "Interpersonal Persuasion in a Vertical Society—The Case of Japan. *Speech Monographs* 38, no. 2 (1971): 148–154.

Osgood, Charles E. "Semantic Differential Technique in the Comparative Study of Cultures." *American Anthropologist* 66 (1964):171–200.

Patterson, William D. "Landmark for World Travel." *World Travel* 97/98 (1970):24.

Peisach, Estelle Cherry. "Children's Comprehension of Teacher and Peer Speech." *Child Development* 36 (1965):467–480.

Pierce, John R. "Communication." *Scientific American* 227, no. 3 (1972): 30–41.

"Proclamation of Tourism Year of the Americas." *World Travel* 104 (1971): 28.

"Protection of Mankind's Cultural Heritage—Sites and Monuments." Paris: UNESCO, 1970.

Pugwash Continuing Committee. "SALT and International Security." *Bulletin of the Atomic Scientists* (December 1971):17–19.

"Recreation Organizers Need Sound Training." *World Travel* 106 (1972): 33–35.

Sarles, Harvey B. "New Approaches to the Study of Human Communication." *Anthropological Linguistics* 8, no. 9 (1966):20–26.

Schatzman, Leonard, and Strauss, Anselm. "Social Class and Modes of Communication." *American Journal of Sociology* 60 (1955):329–338.

Sigel, Irving E., and Perry, Cereta. "Psycholinguistic Diversity Among 'Culturally Deprived' Children." *American Journal of Orthopsychiatry* 38 (1968):122–126.

Sirota, David. "The Multinational Corporation: Management Myths." *Personnel* (January/February 1972):34–41.

Sirota, David, and Greenwood, J. Michael. "Understand Your Overseas Work Force." *Harvard Business Review* (January/February 1971):53–60.

Spolsky, Bernard. "Attitudinal Aspects of Second Language Learning." *Language Learning* 19 (1969):271–285.

Svalastoga, Kaare. "Elite and Social System." *Acta Sociologica* 12 (1969): 13–19.

Tanaka, Yasumasa. "Psychological Factors in International Persuasion." *Annals of the American Academy of Political and Social Science* 398 (1971):50–60.

Taylor, Donald M., and Gardner, Robert C. "Bicultural Communication: A Study of Communicational Efficiency and Person Perception." *Canadian Journal of Behavioral Science* 2 (1970):67–81.

Thant, U. "Can Scholars Succeed Where Diplomats Have Failed? Part I." *World* 1, no. 3 (1972):32–34.

Thant, U. "Can Scholars Succeed Where Diplomats Have Failed? Part II." *World* 1, no. 5 (1972):38–39.

Thiagarajan, K. M., and Deep, Samuel D. "A Study of Supervisor–Subordinate Influence and Satisfaction in Four Cultures." *The Journal of Social Psychology* 82 (1970):173–180.

Triandis, Harry C., and others. "Interpersonal Attitudes Among American, Indian, and Japanese Students." *International Journal of Psychology* 1, no. 3 (1966):177–206.

Tsuzaki, Stanley M., and Reinecke, John E. "English in Hawaii: An Annotated Bibliography." *Oceanic Linguistics*, Special Publication no. 1, 1966.

United Nations. "Declaration of the Principles of International Cultural Co-operation." *Human Rights* (1967): 92–93.

United Nations. *The United Nations and Human Rights.* New York: United Nations, 1968.

Upshur, John A. "Four Experiments on the Relation Between Foreign Language Teaching and Learning." *Language Learning* 18 (1968):111–124.

Useem, John, et al. "Men in the Middle of the Third Culture: The Roles of American and Non-Western People in Cross-Cultural Administration." *Human Organization* 22 (1963):169–179.

Wallenstein, Gerd D. "International Telecommunications, Where 'Co-operation' is the Message." *Telecommunication Journal* 39, no. 6 (1972): 365–370.

Wedge, Bryant. "Training for a Psychiatry of International Relations." *American Journal of Psychiatry* 125 (1968):43–48.

Wilson, Edward O. "Animal Communication." *Scientific American* 227, no. 3 (1972):52–60.

Wilson, Stewart W. "Interactive Lectures." *Technology Review* (January 1972):50–57.

Wolfe, D. L. "Some Theoretical Aspects of Language Learning and Language Teaching." *Language Learning* 17 (1967):173–188.

"The World's Telephones as of January 1, 1972." *AT&T Long Lines*, 1972.

Wooster, Harold, moderator. "Communication with Extra-Terrestrial Intelligence." *IEEE Spectrum* 3, no. 3 (1966):153–163.

Name Index

Subject Index